Pursuing Wealthspan

How Science is Revolutionizing Wealth Management

S. Jay Olshansky, Ph.D.
Kirk Ashburn
Jeff Stukey
(Editors)

Copyright © 2020 S. Jay Olshansky, Kirk Ashburn, Jeff Stukey
All rights reserved.
ISBN: 9798651985449

CONTENTS

Preface   5
Ken Dychtwald

Foreword   9
Kirk Ashburn

Introduction (From Wealth Management)   11
Kirk Ashburn

Introduction (From Aging Science)   16
S. Jay Olshansky

I.   The Wealthspan Message

Chapter 1. The Origin of Wealthspan   19
S. Jay Olshansky, Kirk Ashburn, Jeff Stukey

II.   The Science

Chapter 2. We Need A New Map of Life   31
Jialu Streeter, Matteo Leombroni, Martha Deevy
and Laura Carstensen

Chapter 3. Is 100 the New Life Expectancy for
People Born in the 21st Century?   42
S. Jay Olshansky and Steven N. Austad

Chapter 4. Jeanne Calment Lived to 122:
Should You Plan to Live This Long?   52
S. Jay Olshansky

Chapter 5. Gender and Longevity: Are Women
"Programmed" to Live Longer Than Men   57
Steven N. Austad

Chapter 6. Lifespan Differences Between Spouses
Should Drive Investment Strategies: A Case Study   65
S. Jay Olshansky

III. The Intersection of Wealth Management And Aging Science

Chapter 7. You are not Average! Your Scientifically Determined Lifespan and Healthspan are the Foundation for Your Financial Plan — 77
S. Jay Olshansky

Chapter 8. Managing Your Investments for the Long Haul – How to Keep it Simple — 85
Derek Prusa

Chapter 9. Uncovering a Hidden Asset to Increase Wealthspan — 109
Jay Jackson

Chapter 10. The Importance of a Financial Plan — 125
Ben Webster

Chapter 11. Tax Planning — 147
Kirk Ashburn and Jeff Stukey

Chapter 12. Better Planning Works — 169
Theodore M. Homa

Chapter 13. Life as a Wealthspan Client and Advisor — 175
Jeff Stukey and Kirk Ashburn

Concluding Remarks — 182

Acknowledgments — 185

ABOUT THE AUTHORS — 186

Preface

Ken Dychtwald

The Retirement Health/Wealth Convergence

The fast-growing ranks of American retirees need to find new ways to fund longer retirements, and many are worried about their ability to do so. They don't know the full cost of retirement or how much they need to save, but most save far less than they should.

Three major forces are transforming the challenge of funding retirement. First, longevity continues to climb. The average life expectancy at birth is up to 78 years and is projected to continue to rise, adding nearly two+ years per decade. However, the average retirement age is little changed. That means more retirees will need to fund longer retirements. Second, the massive Baby Boomer retirement wave is dramatically increasing the retiree population, adding about 10,000 new retirees a day. The U.S. population age 65+ will continue its dramatic rise, increasing by half over the next 30 years.

Third, the retirement funding formula is shifting dramatically. Most employers have discontinued guaranteed defined benefit pensions in favor of 401(k) and other forms of defined contribution accounts. And, due to demographic challenges, the long-term viability of Social Security benefits is in question.

Americans need more funding for longer retirements, yet the "three-legged stool" traditionally used for funding retirement—Social Security, employer pension, personal savings—is getting very wobbly for many people. Most of us will need to rely more on personal sources of income, and so the responsibility for managing retirement funding resides more than ever with the individual – and for that, we're grossly unprepared.

Americans are rightly concerned about funding a comfortable retirement, yet most aren't aware of what it will cost. Compared to life's other biggest expenses—buying a home, raising a child, paying for college—retirement carries the highest average price tag.

Many big variables go into financial planning for retirement. How much income per year do I need to live comfortably? How much can I save before retiring? How might my investments perform? The biggest unknown variables are how long each of us will live in retirement and how healthy or sick we'll be in our later years. The answers are different for each of us; however, the uncertainty about getting them right affects almost everyone. Yet, eighty-one percent of Americans report that they don't know how much money they'll need to fund their retirement.

Today's retirees tell us that the #1 ingredient for a happy retirement is health, which can have a far-reaching impact on quality of life, family relationships, and financial security. At the same time, the uncertain and potentially high cost of health care is their #1 financial worry of retirement. This worry far outweighs concerns about stock market performance and tax rates. To complicate matters further, people lack confidence in their financial decisions, and they are the ones that people second guess the most.

Health: The Retirement Planning Wildcard

Holistic planning for retirement must include anticipating and preparing for potential health and long-term care costs. However, healthcare is often a missing link in retirement planning. Age Wave's studies have shown that fewer than one in six pre-retirees (15%) have ever attempted to estimate how much money they might need for health care and long-term care in retirement. Only 42% have health care directives.

As more and more of us live well into our third age, resolving this situation requires a new approach. It requires new knowledge, new attitudes, and new tools for a far smarter and more disciplined management of finances to last a lifetime.

In this timely book, S. Jay Olshansky and Kirk Ashburn share a deep and far-reaching examination of the emerging intersections between longevity, precision medicine and financial planning. Their ideas about how each individual can more intelligently model their own longevity future is both inspired and sorely needed. This book has the potential to save millions of lives.

Ken Dychtwald PhD, CEO of Age Wave, author of seventeen books including, *Age Wave, Healthy Aging, A New Purpose: Redefining Money, Family, Work, Retirement and Success* and his long-awaited new book *What Retirees Want: A Holistic View of Life's Third Age* (7/15/20).

Foreword

Kirk Ashburn

In May of 2019 I was sitting with my wife in the surgery prep area at a hospital waiting to be wheeled in for a non-life-threatening procedure. My wife turned to me and asked how much life insurance I have and what she should do if something happens to me. Not exactly the conversation I was hoping for at that moment. She didn't think our coverage was sufficient for her and the kids. I assured her this is just a routine procedure, so don't worry.

I was dead wrong. Three days in an ICU from a mistake that almost had me bleed to death made me look at planning for my future a little differently.

We cannot know in advance exactly how much time will pass after retirement, but we can proactively plan in advance as a gift to ourselves and the people left behind.

'The time for planning is now', if my story isn't evidence enough. And it's not just the peace of mind that comes with a well thought out retirement plan; it's the gifts of financial security and the life-long pursuit of health and happiness for all of my clients that brings me to work every day. This is why the idea behind the rise of Wealthspan has already had such an impact on my life. I want to fundamentally change the way in which families look at and plan for their future. If you fail to plan, you might as well plan to fail.

We hope you enjoy reading Pursuing Wealthspan as much as we enjoyed writing it. Take action now; take care of yourself and your loved ones; enjoy life to the fullest, because time and health might very well be the most precious gifts of all.

Introduction
(From Wealth Management)

Kirk Ashburn

There's a scene in the movie Godfather II when the wealthy businessman Hyman Roth – suffering from prostate issues that were largely untreatable at the time – declares that he would give up all of his accumulated wealth just to be healthy again. This view that health is more important than longevity has been supported in multiple scientific publications through the years. If people are given a choice on where to spend their hard-earned dollars – and there is a choice between health extension and life extension without regard to health – healthy life is by far the first choice. This makes intuitive sense, of course, because it's hard to imagine that anyone wants to experience an extended period of frailty just to remain alive.

Roth was echoing the sentiment that seems to be shared universally, which is that health and happiness (and the time to enjoy them) are indeed the most precious commodities that exist. Whatever you can do during the course of life to develop and preserve them are the foundation of how to live today and plan for the future. Once health and happiness are lost, it no longer matters how much money you have.

We've also come to realize that our clients make decisions about saving for retirement during the course of life that have a profound influence on their chances of maintaining their health and happiness into old age. In the case of Hyman Roth, ensuring that he managed his wealth wisely might have been the approach taken by his wealth advisors when he was younger, but it clearly did not make him happy in his old age because he lost something of great value. While your wealth advisor is no substitute for a personal physician, what an advisor can do is first help you navigate the difficult task of determining what health and happiness mean for you, and then identify the tools of wealth management most likely to help you achieve and preserve this vision of the future.

Financial Advising Today

When you meet with your financial advisor today, the common approach to assessing the future is for the advisor to ask you how long you think you're going to live. Sometimes they don't even ask this question; and instead just assume the same survival estimate for everyone sitting on the other side of the desk. A slightly more sophisticated wealth advisor might ask for your age, and then they'll look up your estimated lifespan from a generic life table – a set of numbers drawn from the observed survival experience of everyone in the population. This is better than not asking anything personal about you at all, but not by much. Some advisors will even use what sounds like a sophisticated tool called a "Monte Carlo simulation" – a computer program designed to estimate a retirement age or to orchestrate a probability of success in having financial assets left over at the end of life.

These decisions (and computer models) are all generated based on one critical assumption – that *you're just like the average man or woman in the U.S.* There is no accounting for what is unique about you that could lead to a much longer or shorter life than average, such as the effect of education, health and disease history, behavioral risk factors such as smoking or physical activity, family history or genetic makeup, or a myriad of other personal attributes known to influence how long you're likely to live.

This approach to advising is used out of sheer force of habit. Until now, advisors never had the tools needed to separate you from average, so it was just easier to use averaging assumptions. The problem with "averaging" assumptions is that your actual lifespan has a 95% chance of being different from such an estimate. Imagine how an incorrect lifespan estimate might influence the outcome of your decision on when to receive Social Security retirement income, and how long that income will last?

A revolution in wealth management is taking place. It is now possible to help clients create a realistic personalized picture of their unique health and survival attributes based on scientifically verified methods of assessment – and the answers are available in minutes, not months. The goal is to:

- Maximize your chances of achieving a condition we refer to as "*Positive Wealthspan*" (defined by the attributes below) by correctly identifying what separates you from average;
- Help you identify your goals for health and happiness;
- Generate a personalized assessment of your survival and health prospects;
- Match your financial resources to this personalized assessment and stated goals;
- Develop a plan so your wealth outlasts your lifespan;
- Leave behind a predetermined financial legacy to your family;
- And most importantly of all, maximize your health and happiness and achieve peace of mind that you planned the best way possible.

A "Neutral Wealthspan" is when you achieve everything above except leaving behind a financial legacy; and a "Negative Wealthspan" is when you outlive your financial resources and/or lose the precious commodities of health and happiness. The focus of this book is on how to achieve and enhance *"Positive Wealthspan"*, so these former two conditions will not be discussed further.

The title of this book exemplifies our primary goal, which is to revolutionize the way in which wealth management is done in order to achieve *Positive Wealthspan*. Who benefits? Clients can now make work, retirement, and some health decisions based on personalized assessments of health and longevity that were previously not possible to generate. Financial advisors now have a new set of tools at their disposal that are easy to use and understand by both them and their clients – enabling them to personalize wealth management, expand their client base, and justify their wealth management recommendations with science-based information. Insurance companies and banks that create wealth management products should see a significant increase in their adoption. In other words, everyone benefits.

You're about to learn how science is disrupting the wealth management industry.

Introduction
(From Aging Science)

S. Jay Olshansky

Planning for retirement in 1900 was easy. Back then, most people didn't live long enough to retire from their life's work as we do routinely today, or they barely made enough money to live day-to-day, let alone save for the future. The last 120 years brought forth an unprecedented longevity revolution that changed everything.

Life used to be lived in just two or three phases: birth and early life development up to age 10; followed by education (although historically many people skipped this phase out of necessity and went to work as teenagers); and then family and work occupied the remainder of life. The concept of retirement as we know it today, which often includes a significant part of life lived after the working phase of life ends, was nonexistent throughout most of human history.

The longevity revolution of the 20th century changed everything. The gift of longevity was manufactured by medicine and science – providing an additional 30 years to the average lifespan across much of the globe. As a result, many are now expected to live into a new phase of life after work ends (e.g., post retirement). Today, some people are living upwards of one-third of their lives in retirement.

Dr. Ken Dychtwald – one of the world's leading experts on human aging, refers to this gift of time as "Life's Third Age" in his new book *What Retirees Want*. Dr. Laura Carstensen from the Stanford University Center on Aging describes this transition to longer lives and its implications, and our need to change the way we think about and plan for our extended lives, as "A New Map of Life". We agree with both visionaries. This newly elongated later phase of life that rarely existed for generations before us, requires a modern set of planning tools and options that are uniquely designed.

We have public health and modern medicine to thank for the gifts of our extended lives and the opportunity to retire and enjoy another phase of life, and you can rest assured that both are still working hard to manufacture even more survival and retirement time for us – hopefully in good health. They are likely to be successful, so planning for longer and healthier lives now is more important than ever.

The challenge is, many have not prepared appropriately for this later phase of life. Most are not aware of advances in medicine and public health that are likely to influence their health and longevity going forward. Few wealth managers are knowledgeable about new methods of assessing longevity and health risks. And almost no one recognizes the survival differences between spouses or partners that are built into our biology; including the folks who most need to be aware of these differences - the clients of financial advisors trying to plan for a secure financial future.

Section I. The Wealthspan Message

Chapter 1. The Origin of Wealthspan

S. Jay Olshansky and Kirk Ashburn

In 2001, two scientists in the field of aging placed a bet that has gone down in scientific circles as one of the most famous wagers ever made. The question at the heart of this bet was, would anyone alive in the year 2000 still be alive and cognitively intact in the year 2150? If yes, someone would have to live for at least 150 years – 28 years longer than the world record of 122 years set by a French woman by the name of Jeanne Calment who died at age 122 in 1997.

Steve Austad from the University of Alabama took one side of the bet supporting the claim that someone will survive to age 150 by 2050. The other side of the bet was taken by me. Whoever wins this bet becomes fabulously wealthy because at least $1 billion goes to the winner. What's the catch? Neither Austad nor I expect to be alive in 2150, so the winner will be one or more of our surviving relatives – but the $1 billion is real money [https://www.sciencemag.org/news/2001/02/long-lived-bet.].

Where did Steve and I come up with $1 billion to make this bet? The answer is simple – the magic of compound interest. We started out in the year 2001 with a $300 investment ($150 each) and doubled it some 15 years later. The money was first invested in gold at $800/oz and sold at $1,500/oz; then it was moved into the stock market where all of it was invested in Tesla. The investment outperformed once again. However, most of the $1 billion available in 2150 will be a byproduct of patience. An update on this bet appears in Chapter 2.

The lessons learned from this wager speak to the value of retirement planning because most of the money used to pay off this bet will accrue from compound interest on the original investment. While patience is an important lesson for investors of all ages, a financial planner saw much more to this bet than meets the eye. Kirk Ashburn, the architect that created Wealthspan Financial Partners, has been a financial planner since 2002 – having served his clients well for many years. He became frustrated by the lack of innovation and the same old tired products being repackaged in new ways by the companies that offer them. It's no wonder, he thought, that it's so difficult getting people of all ages to plan for their future.

Knowledge of this wager changed everything for him. In all of his years as a wealth advisor, the most important lesson learned was what Hyman Roth articulated so well in The

Godfather movie – that the most precious commodities sought by his clients are, by far, health and happiness. Longevity is just a bonus. Wealth is a catalyst that can amplify the chances both will occur, and longevity is a gift as long as it's accompanied by good health.

Recognizing the combined importance of health, longevity, happiness, and wealth, Kirk coined the term *Wealthspan* to exemplify the merging of aging science with wealth planning. In order to launch this idea as a new science based advisory firm (mywealthspan.com), he sought the scientific guidance of myself and Steve Austad and the expertise of the scientific team I assembled as the cofounder and chief scientist at Lapetus Solutions where novel assessments of healthspan and lifespan have been developed. The result is a fresh well validated science-based set of tools and products that are being formulated especially for them – designed to transform the world of financial planning with a central focus on only one thing; enhancing the "Positive Wealthspan" of his clients.

Instead of using antiquated methods of wealth planning that date back centuries, which are still used today throughout the financial services industries, advisors can now create personalized assessments of health and longevity based on aging science that are designed to help people understand and plan for their future in ways that are unprecedented in the industry. To appreciate the importance of this breakthrough, let's look back in time to the way things have always been done in the world of financial planning.

Stage I Assessments (18th and 19th century technology)

In the early 19th century a British actuary set out to discover a mathematical formula that insurance companies could use to set premiums for life insurance. The question he needed to answer was simple – what is the relationship between age and the risk of death? While it was already known then that the longer you live the greater your chance of dying in the coming year (the first life table was developed in 1693 by Edmund Halley), insurance companies needed mathematical precision.

Gompertz set out to meticulously collect data on the longevity of people across Europe by age and gender, and discovered a simple formula that accurately portrayed a pattern of death for people between the ages of 20 and 80. Gompertz's observation that the risk of death doubles about every 8 years after age 20 was so consistent across populations and time periods that it became the standard in the life insurance industry for setting premiums. This link between age and risk of death has since become known as the "law of mortality", and it's still in use today.

The Gompertz mortality "law" was eventually discovered to apply to many other species from worms to weasels to wombats, so to speak, not just humans. Another general pattern, overlaying the Gompertz law which applies to populations, is that *individual* life trajectories are diverse. That is, among people born on the same day or year, even among those living their entire lives in similar circumstances, some will live long, some will die early, but most will live an intermediate length of time. This consistent pattern occurs even among genetically identical mice living in identical cages eating identical diets living in identical rooms from birth to death. This means that there is a random element to aging that cannot be controlled, and it applies to people just as it applies to other living things like mice and elephants.

The reason the Gompertz formula is so consistent in its ability to predict survival patterns in populations is because it is based on principles of biology suggesting that the genetic configuration of almost all living things is heavily influenced by the environments in which each species arose. These environments, in turn, govern how long it takes each generation to mature and have children of their own.

Growth, development, and maturation are driven by genetically fixed programs inherited by every member of each species, and how long people and other organisms live is calibrated to these traits – known as life history traits. Insurance companies rely heavily on this regularity in the pattern of death, and the original Gompertz formula from 1825 has been used effectively by insurance companies and annuitants for nearly 200 years; and to some extent, it is still in use today.

Advisors often base his/her retirement plan for their clients entirely on age, gender, and financial status; and accumulated current and anticipated future assets stretched out over a hypothetical age that is generically applied to everyone (such as age 95). If your advisor doesn't inquire at all about any of your personal attributes and just recommends investment options, he or she is using what I call a Stage I assessment tool. Stage I assessment and advice technologies in wealth management are still commonly used today, and in my view, they belong in the 19th century where they originated.

Stage II Assessments

In the 20th century, advances in medical science and public health extended both the healthspan of individuals and the life expectancy of populations at a breathtaking pace.

Yet the Gompertz Law held steady – the risk of death still doubles about every 8 years today, in spite of life expectancy at birth rising by 30 years since 1900. Nevertheless, insurance companies now know certain attributes of individuals can be predictive of longer or shorter lives. The most common predictors now in use include smoking status and body mass index (BMI). As a result, the Society of Actuaries created separate "life tables" for people with these attributes, and the U.S. Social Security Administration created generic life tables based on the mortality experience of the entire resident population of the U.S.

What this means is that financial advisors now have a somewhat more advanced tool at their disposal to help them assess survival prospects for their clients. You can now go into your advisor's office, and he/she can ask you your age and simply open up a book or computer screen and look up your estimated remaining lifespan on a spreadsheet. How easy is that? I refer to these tools as Stage II technologies and they're certainly better than using nothing at all, but not by much. They at least yield some valuable information that is similar to what insurance companies use to place people into risk pools.

The bad news is that this form of assessment is based on VERY LARGE generic pools using population statistics that are designed to create averages. The probability that you'll fall within the narrow range of lifespan estimates is actually quite small – usually about 5%. This means there is about a 95% chance that you'll live longer or shorter than an estimate derived from generic life tables.

There are few things less personal than assuming you're average; using statistics based on national averages to support this view; and then developing a plan for your average financial future based on the most often incorrect assumption that you're average. This is particularly problematic when it comes to financial planning because the distance between being average and residing on either end of the survival distribution, or even one standard deviation away from average, is almost always enough to have a material impact on how you plan for your future life in retirement.

Stage II assessment tools are better than not using anything at all, but one thing you can be sure of – you are unlikely to be average. If you're a financial advisor reading this, your clients are equally unlikely to be average!

Stage III Assessments

What makes each person unique – even among genetically identical twins – is that people acquire highly unique experiences during their lives that reverberate throughout life that influence health and survival. For example, although identical twins share the same genome at birth, if one of them smokes cigarettes and the other does not, this one experience alone can have a dramatic effect on the relative expected survival of the twins.

Take a look at the image of identical twins in Figure 1 – one of whom smokes and the other does not. Science demonstrates that the twin with the more advanced face age – which is clearly visible in the photograph – will have earlier and more age-related diseases and a shorter lifespan relative to her identical twin. Examples of just a few other powerful inherited and acquired risk factors that separate you from average include years of completed education, financial stability, smoking status, body mass index, family history of longevity, level of physical activity, among many others. Now you know why some people live so long while others die at younger ages – even among identical twins.

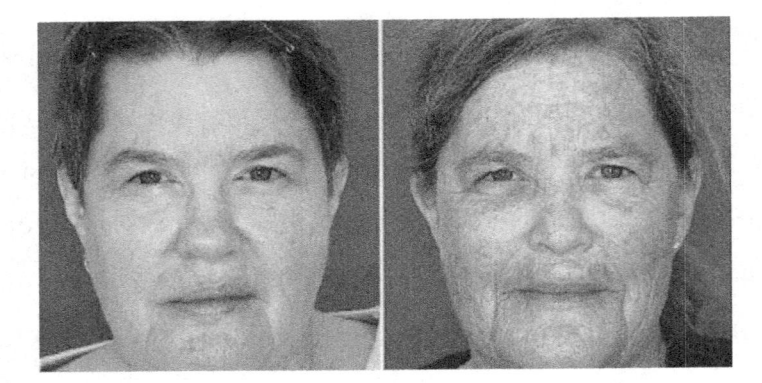

Figure 1. Identical smoker/nonsmoker twins. For an excellent summary showing a number of examples just like this, go here [Okada, Haruko C. M.D.; Alleyne, Brendan B.S.; Varghai, Kaveh; Kinder, Kimberly M.D.; Guyuron, Bahman M.D. Facial Changes Caused by Smoking, Plastic and Reconstructive Surgery: November 2013 - Volume 132 - Issue 5 - p 1085-1092 doi: 10.1097/PRS.0b013e3182a4c20a]

Now consider the importance of genes. Increasingly sophisticated epidemiology combined with the accumulation of more detailed data on massively greater numbers of people have led to an enhanced ability to make predictions about health and longevity among groups of people with certain genetic traits. For example, one well-documented genetic variant (called an "allele") that is associated with a higher probability of living to ages 90 and older is the FOXO3 gene. If you're a carrier of one of favorable versions of this allele, your chance of making it to 100 is about 50% higher than non-carriers. While inheriting this allele is not a guarantee for a long life (because favorable longevity genes can easily be overcome by harmful risk factors like smoking), knowing that you are a carrier could (and should) influence how you plan for your financial future.

An allele associated with a higher risk of late onset Alzheimer's disease – APOE – is also one of the more well studied alleles known to influence both length and quality of life. One variant of the APOE allele is associated with a longer and healthier life in old age while a different one increases the probability of late-onset Alzheimer's disease. With genetic analysis entering into the picture, it now becomes possible to leverage new tools of aging science to help wealth managers guide their clients toward retirement products that more closely align with personal inherited and acquired life circumstances that are currently invisible to wealth managers stuck using Stage I and Stage II assessment tools.

The good news from our perspective is that science can actually measure and quantify the influence of most of these acquired and inherited attributes; and the process of measuring them takes only a few minutes. Science makes it possible to generate personalized health and longevity assessments that are not otherwise visible, and which allow for the development of financial planning strategies with strikingly greater precision than ever before – revolutionizing wealth management.

- Regulators that oversee the wealth management industry to ensure clients are receiving advice that is in their best interest, can justify backing these scientific approaches to wealth management assessment because they're based on published verifiable evidence that has gone through rigorous peer review;
- Wealth advisors now have science-based tools at their disposal that, when presented to their clients, illustrate precisely what is unique about them and how and why their plans for the future could and should make use of this valuable information;
- Clients will not only learn something new about themselves they were previously unaware of; they will also understand what makes them unique. This knowledge drives the customized wealth management plan that advisors are developing on their behalf.

II. The Science
Chapter 2. We Need A New Map of Life

Jialu Streeter, Matteo Leombroni, Martha Deevy and Laura Carstensen

The dramatic increase in the likelihood of reaching old age is among the greatest cultural achievements in human history. In the U.S., life expectancy rose from 47 years in 1900 to 79 years in 2020. Life expectancy at 65 continues to increase today.

Yet, we are failing to think creatively about ways to use longer lives to improve quality of life. In our view, we will not take full advantage of longer lives until we adopt a life course perspective that recognizes the complexity of financial planning, the unique challenges faced by women and members of minority groups, how early decisions about work and family ripple throughout life, and the perniciousness of debt. People do not find themselves financially comfortable or insecure in old age by chance. Rather, the paths on which we travel through life – whether because of choices we make or due to our place in society – determine whether or not we achieve financial security in late life.

From a life course perspective, there are troubling trends:
- Half of Americans report that they do not feel financially secure.
- Median family net worth in 2013 was less than median family net worth in 1989.
- Americans approaching retirement in 2016 had saved less, but borrowed more, than near-retirees in the early 1990s.
- The average retirement age of men today is the same as that in 1962.
- In 2005, Americans, on average, saved a mere 2.2 percent of disposable personal income, compared to 13 percent in the 1970s and less than many other developed countries.
- In 2019, 12 percent of American households said they could not cover an unexpected expense of $400, and 27 percent would have to borrow the money or sell something they owned.

Stanford Center on Longevity's New Map of Life initiative is premised on the belief that long lives present grand opportunities and novel risks. In order to reap the possibilities that longer lives present, every aspect of life will need to change fundamentally: early childhood, healthcare, lifestyles, and the approach to financing long lives. When discussions about financial security are limited to questions about the size of 401k contributions and whether or not to delay retirement by a year or two, we fail to address a larger question, namely, how do we build a culture that supports satisfying lives that could last for a century or more? While we are fully aware of the magnitude of the challenge, a conversation must begin. We will not achieve what we cannot envision.

Our objective in this chapter is to reframe a discussion of financial security to consider the many ways that it interacts with socioeconomic status, work, family, and education. We maintain that these interrelationships must be addressed in order to create social norms, infrastructures, and policies that support long and prosperous lives for the majority of Americans.

Why don't we better plan for our financial futures?

Financial planning was not an issue for most of human history - we didn't live long enough. Individual responsibility for financial planning is newer still. So, it's not surprising that we are failing to prepare. However, we find ourselves living in a world where financial resources affect how we spend our time, provide for our loved ones, chase our dreams, and engage with the world. We need to do better.

Many of the reasons for this lack of preparedness are not economic. They include a desire for immediate gratification, poor self-control, and inertia. In addition, a lack of financial knowledge impairs individuals' abilities to make sound financial decisions. In 2019, only one-third of respondents could answer at least four of five basic financial literacy questions on topics such as mortgage, interest compounding, inflation, and risk. Relatedly, many mistakes are made unwittingly. Failing to maximize tax sheltered retirement savings, taking out loans against retirement plans, and failing to roll over plans with moves from one employer to another, are examples of mistakes that have major ramifications. Low financial competence is related to using high-cost products such as payday loans, failing to pay credit card balances, and also to choices that incur more fees and interest on mortgages, which can lead to excessive debt.

Yet, focusing mostly on individual inadequacies is too limited. Robert Gallucci, former president of the MacArthur Foundation, said, "If you want the American dream, you have to move to the Netherlands." Indeed, recent research has called into question the widespread American belief anyone can achieve financial wellness with hard work and determination. The U.S. is ranked 11th among the G20 countries on social mobility, and our standing in the world is declining over time. Put another way, it takes five generations for a low-income family to reach the median income in the U.S.; in Denmark, it takes two.

Geography matters. Children born into poor neighborhoods in regions of the country with high income inequality, low-quality neighborhood schools, and thin social capital face nearly insurmountable difficulties climbing the income ladder. Furthermore, the ability to save and invest is severely limited by resources that extend beyond individual choices. In low-income households, basic needs such as food, housing, transportation, and health care, consume the lion's share of take-home pay, leaving little to save.

Family matters. Wealth is influenced by family of origin, marriage, and divorce. Family assistance from older generations to their adult children as they are launched from their childhood homes is highly correlated with wealth accumulation. Marriage allows individuals to pool resources, thereby increasing the odds of homeownership which is a core asset for many Americans. Of course, the pooling of resources and shared decision making can be a double-edged sword.

Conflict over money is among the top reasons for divorce, which often reduces financial security, especially for women. And, not surprisingly, financial stress over money is more common among those with limited education and, relatedly, fewer resources. Family resources also matter in times of financial need or hardship. Coming from families that contribute to college tuition or down payments on mortgages is critical to alleviating the debt burden of young adults. In addition to these predictable needs, few families escape unexpected shocks, such as job loss and health issues, and resilience often relies on the financial resources of others, especially parents. Notably, for the majority of life, more money flows down through the generations than up. Children born into relatively affluent families benefit from ongoing parental financial support as adults, which helps them reduce debt and increase wealth.

Gender and race matter. In addition to wage differentials for women and men, as well as majority and minority racial groups, ongoing discrimination affects opportunities to earn. Women are more likely than men to step out of the labor market during the childbearing and childrearing years, reducing their lifetime earnings and retirement savings. Consequently, divorce and widowhood are financial shocks that disproportionately impact women. Women are more likely to be caregivers in later life, spending down assets while caring for spouses, and jeopardizing their own future security. Many members of racial minority groups face cumulative disadvantages throughout life, from education, career choices, earnings and savings, to health outcomes. Here too, financial status of prior generations influences the degree to which parents are able to assist their adult children to establish themselves, thus perpetuating differences between more and less affluent families over historical time.

The financial benefit system matters. Currently, access to 401(k)-type plans and affordable health insurance are tied to employment, and therefore, socioeconomic class. Millions of working Americans, mostly self-employed, part-time, or gig workers, have no access to a 401(k) or low-cost healthcare insurance. The Affordable Care Act (ACA) expanded health insurance coverage but failed to reduce the cost. The SECURE Act passed in December 2019 offers hope for millions of Americans to save for retirement by lifting prior restrictions on plan eligibility and making retirement plans more accessible to more people. The outcomes of these programs are still unfolding.

Accumulating wealth while managing debt is increasingly challenging and uncertain

A generation ago, homeownership was a financial milestone that constituted an essential component of family wealth accumulation. Owning a home not only provided stable shelter and grounding in local communities. The eventual sale of a home owned outright offered an important complement to retirement savings. By the time people retired, housing debt was limited. Homeownership was part of the glide path to financial security.

For a host of reasons, owning a home has become increasingly difficult. Compared to Baby Boomers, Millennials are less likely to own a home by age 30. Even among homeowners, they shoulder a substantial housing debt burden. Between 1970 and 2010, outstanding mortgage debt in the U.S, grew 32 times, while the cost of consumer goods grew only six times. Fewer people today pay off home loans by retirement: the percentage of older households carrying a mortgage rose from 24% in 1970 to 46% in 2016. A high level of indebtedness threatens the retirement security of millions of older Americans by reducing their personal finances and heightening housing and food insecurity.

Arguably, ripple effects from early to late life are best illustrated by student loan debt. The cost of going to college doubled between 1990 and 2020 (adjusted for inflation), leaving an average graduate today with over $30,000 in debt. While there is ample evidence for the positive contribution's education makes to health, well-being, and lifetime earnings, student loan debt is now second only to mortgage debt in American families, and the consequences for financial security are alarming.

Accumulating significant student loans can result in making career choices based largely on pay, which may not maximize a person's talent and potential over the long run. Heavy debt delays marriage and home ownership. The sharp reduction in homeownership rate post-2008 crisis was particularly severe for households with student debt. When a substantial share of paychecks goes to student debt, young people have little choice but to put off saving for retirement. Late payments or defaulting on student loans lower one's credit score, resulting in higher interest rates on credit cards, auto loans, and mortgages.

The final blow comes for many in the reduction of Social Security benefits. The federal government can garnish up to 15 percent of Social Security benefits for those who defaulted on student debts. In the fiscal year 2015 alone, almost 114,000 borrowers age 50 and older had Social Security benefits seized to repay defaulted federal student loans.

Unlike credit card debt, it is very difficult for student loans to be cleared through bankruptcy. Thus, the debt burden can have long-term implications for wealth accumulation. Compared to their debt-free peers with similar educations, individuals who borrowed to pursue higher education accumulate less in-home equity, financial wealth, cash, and net wealth.

Summary

Thirty years were added to life expectancy in the 20th century, representing what is arguably the greatest cultural achievement in human history. More time can allow people to live higher quality lives: we can stretch out childhood, spend more time with our families, engage more with communities, and work more years but fewer hours in a week. Reaching the potential of century-long lives demands innovative thinking about financing long lives.

There are roles for public and private insurance that can cushion financial shocks, novel savings vehicles that reduce cumulative disadvantage, financial products that incentivize savings, risk sharing products that allow people to share their lots, and innovative thinking about financial literacy.

We maintain that retirement security and *Positive Wealthspan* will not be achieved without recognition of influences that begin long before people open retirement savings accounts.

Chapter 3. Is 100 the New Life Expectancy for People Born in the 21st Century?

S. Jay Olshansky and Steven N. Austad

Recall the longevity bet that Kirk and Jeff read about that got their attention? Well, in February of 2020, Steve and I were contacted by a reporter from the Wall Street Journal (WSJ) about a story she wanted to write on any new developments in the bet and its relevance for today. There have been numerous stories written about this bet over the last 20 years, but I think this story best exemplifies our current thinking on this issue and its relevance for today. I've provided below the full story that appeared in the WSJ on the 20th of April in 2020.

Stephen N. Austad: The Leap Will Come from Focusing on Aging Itself

People born in the 21st century – today's college students, for instance – can expect to live a century or more because their health will be unlike anything seen before in human history. This new surge in life expectancy will not be due to doctors becoming better at diagnosing and treating the diseases that kill us today. It will be due to our new ability to prevent and delay most or all of the diseases and disabilities that plague later life.

During the 20th century, life expectancy in the U.S. surged some 63%, to 77 years from 48. That progress was driven by better hygiene, the development of vaccines and antibiotics, and later on, better diagnosis and treatments of individual diseases. Similar progress in the 21st century will easily take us to a 100-year lifespan.

We'll get there, but not by focusing as we have in the past on one disease at a time. Near the past century's end, the new approach to health began to emerge, focused not on diseases themselves, but on the underlying processes of aging itself. Aging is the biggest risk factor in virtually everything that kills us today.

Beginning with tiny round worms and fruit flies, researchers discovered that treating aging as if it were a disease was not difficult. We could do it by altering genes, modifying diets and, most surprisingly, with the use of some existing drugs developed for other purposes. These treatments worked not only in the simplest animals; they also worked in mice – mammals like us.

Geroscientists – a new word for a new field – have found that treating aging has remarkably broad benefits. One drug, for instance, rapamycin, has made mice live considerably longer. It has delayed some mouse cancers and completely eliminated others; it also has delayed mouse versions of Alzheimer's disease, heart disease and the advance of forgetfulness of later life. And in a limited study involving humans, a drug closely related to rapamycin was seen to have benefits for people 65 and older in the form of improved protection from flu when used in combination with a flu vaccine.

Then came a truly unexpected discovery. Rapamycin had virtually the same health benefits whether started later in a mouse's life – the mouse equivalent of 60 - 75 years old – or early.

It's true, the biology of mice and humans differs. But we share 98% of the same genes. Meanwhile, another drug, metformin, for treating diabetes, shows promise in preventing or delaying the maladies of aging. Moreover, the drug has shown more promise in studies involving humans than it has in mouse studies. The many studies involving humans compared people taking metformin for diabetes with people not taking metformin, or taking another diabetes drug, and compared the rates of cancer, heart disease and dementia in those groups. The studies found less frequent incidence of these illnesses in the groups taking metformin than in the groups not taking it. Discoveries of this sort are emerging at a faster and faster pace.

It's true, adding just one year of life expectancy is more difficult the older one gets. With 80 years behind you, for example, and various age-related illnesses lining up before you, the odds of reaching 100 worsen. But we have to stop thinking about age-related diseases as independent entities. Diseases associated with aging have extensively overlapping causes, so that a treatment (like rapamycin) affects most or all such ailments. Treating aging itself thus can dramatically change the mortality rates currently seen in our later years. Hundreds of life-extending animal experiments show that what we previously thought of as "limits" can be burst through with the right treatment.

No one should rush to get prescriptions or try out aging-retarding therapies before they are properly evaluated for safety and efficacy in people. But testing has started.

We don't know yet which of the various health-extending treatments for aging that work so unequivocally in mice will work in people too, but we will. And the early evidence suggests that those treatments, even if they aren't available until mid-century or later, can still extend lives and health like nothing we have ever seen before.

S. Jay Olshansky: Blame it on Math, Science, Common Sense and Our Bodies

Predicting that children born in the U.S. from 2000 on will have a life expectancy of at least 100 is nothing short of radical – but not for the reasons you might think.

Our understanding of the biology of aging will advance; breakthroughs are on the horizon that will slow the effects of aging; the extension of healthy life will soon transform what it means to grow old; and Nobel prizes await the scientists who make this possible.

Life expectancy will inch up, to well short of 100 – but the Holy Grail of what I call extended healthspan will finally be realized. Let's stop striving for an unattainable goal of radical life extension, or, worse, claiming it has already arrived. Common sense dictates that we shift the focus of medicine and public health to extending that part of our later lives in which we enjoy good health.

The problem with the idea of living routinely to 100 is that math, science, common sense and our inherited body "design" get in the way.

The first longevity revolution – the 30-year increase in life expectancy seen in the 20th century – occurred mostly because of declining early age mortality thanks to advances in public health. This was boosted later in the century by reductions in death rates at middle and older ages as lifestyles improved, and because of new methods of detecting and treating aging-related diseases.

But look where we are today. Even ideal behavioral risk factors won't transform a 70-year-old into a supercentenarian. Conquering aging-related disease one at a time would yield diminishing gains in life expectancy the older one gets.

Perhaps the biggest reason humans can't expect to routinely live to 100 is this: Life expectancy is a population metric, and it gets harder to move the needle the older we get. Adding one year to life expectancy when it is 80 is orders of magnitude more difficult than when it is 50. Attaining a life expectancy of 90 requires the equivalent of cures for cancer, all cardiovascular diseases, diabetes, infectious diseases and accidental deaths. Getting to 95 requires the elimination of all known causes of death short of aging. And getting to 100 requires not only that we slow aging, but the survival time would need to be added to the lives of people age 70+ at a rate faster than it was added to lives of children born at the start of the 20th century.

There can and should be some marginal gains in life expectancy for demographic subgroups; reducing disparities between the rich and poor, for example, is desperately needed. But a second longevity revolution on par with the first is highly unlikely.

One more point on the mathematical argument: the law of averages requires that for 100 to be the new life expectancy, a significant proportion of the population routinely must survive beyond the current maximum lifespan limit 122 – an age known to have been reached by just one person. This alone is sufficient to cast doubt on claims that 100 is the new normal.

Scientists who nevertheless back such claims point to research in which aging has been slowed and lifespans increased in short-lived species. But humans don't experience biological time at the same rate as those species. A doubling of the lifespan of a short-lived species will likely yield only a fraction of that gain in humans. Doubling the lifespan of a mouse from three to six years doesn't mean the lifespan of humans will double from 80 to 160.

Keep in mind that aging interventions aren't seeking to "cure" aging itself. That would be an unrealistic target with no evidence to support it. Aging isn't a disease, any more than growth, development, puberty and menopause are. When aging interventions are eventually introduced, they will likely delay diseases, compress morbidity, extend healthspan and yield economic dividends to individuals and societies. In the final analysis, though, some diseases will recede in favor of others, and the game of disease Whack-A-Mole (referred to as competing risks in epidemiology) will continue.

A better goal than extending human lifespan is the extension of the periods in our lives in which we enjoy good health. Humans are no more capable of routinely living to 100 as a population then we are expected to all run a 4-minute mile, high-jump 8 feet, or dunk a basketball – at least not in these bodies with this body design.

So, there you have it, one of the more famous bets in science from those who made the bet. Interest in this wager extended far and wide, with media coverage about the bet appearing in multiple news and scientific publications over the years. The editor of Wired Magazine was so intrigued by this idea that he created a website called "long bets" [longbets.org] in which scientists and others place friendly wagers – with real money – on a broad range of prospective future events. The winnings in longbets.org go to charitable organizations, but Steve and I chose instead to enhance our genetic lineage by ensuring that the winnings go to our surviving relatives. Exactly what they'll be able to buy in 2150 with $1 billion is uncertain. Perhaps the winner's surviving relatives will have enough cash to buy the loser's surviving relatives a round of drinks to toast their good fortune.

The importance of this story to wealth management advisors and clients is evident. The common theme that runs through these predictions is what Hyman Roth articulated in The Godfather. The most precious commodities are health and happiness. If wealth planning is a tool that can be used to increase the chances of achieving *Positive Wealthspan*, then it doesn't matter which of us wins this bet.

If Steve is correct, then all of us need to plan for longer and healthier lives that could greatly exceed any estimates currently derived through Stage I or Stage II predictive technologies. The good news if Steve is right is that we can anticipate longer lives filled with more good health than is currently predicted by any health forecasting model out there today, and the cost of health care for each of us would likely be significantly reduced.

The bad news – which some will not consider bad – is that we'll all need to make significant adjustments to our wealth plan to ensure that we experience *Positive Wealthspan* during our extended healthy lives. That's right, we would likely have to work longer, delay retirement longer, and stretch out our life's savings for a longer than anticipated time frame.

If I'm right, then we are equally likely to experience longer and healthier lives for the same reasons posited by Steve – just not to the extent he predicts for a single individual that he thinks might live to 150. Since the chances of anyone reading this book will be the one to break the world record for longevity, or even reach 110+, is extremely remote, then the result of the bet itself is a moot point. What's important is that both of us are equally optimistic that aging science is on the verge of a breakthrough that is likely to extend our lifespan and healthspan, and the time is now to begin planning for this.

In the next chapter I'm going to introduce you to the most famous person in the world of aging – the record holder for human longevity. Her story is fascinating because it relates directly to issues of financial planning.

Chapter 4. Jeanne Calment Lived to 122: Should You Plan to Live This Long?

S. Jay Olshansky

The most celebrated case of human longevity is that of Jeanne Louise Calment who was born on 21 February 1875 in Arles, France, and who died on 4 August 1997. This world record holder for human longevity, which formally defines maximum lifespan for our species, lived for 122 years, 164 days.

Figure 2. Jeanne Calment: Photo on the left from 1996, one year before she died. Jeanne smoked for 100 years. This is not a license to smoke – most that do so will die earlier than if a nonsmoker. This just means that smoking was unlikely to have been a significant risk factor for her.

The second longest-lived person was Sarah Knauss from the U.S. who died in 1999 at 119 years, 97 days. There are 14 documented cases of people alive today (as of June 2020) that are aged 110 and older; and the number of centenarians (people aged 100+) has been on the rise for decades and is expected to continue throughout this century. However, most of that increase is due to larger birth rates more than a century ago rather than the miracle powers of medicine extending life by decades for those who otherwise might live only into their 70s or 80s. Should you plan on living to 100 or as high as 122?

In the U.S., the chance that a baby born in 2020 will live to 100 or older is about 3.7% for girls and 1.7% for boys – assuming death rates observed today prevail for the next century. It is a given that medical advances will continue throughout this century, so we can optimistically assume that the probabilities are actually closer to 5% -10% for most babies born today. If you're already in the 40-80 age range, the chance you'll make it to 100 is actually a bit lower than my optimistic 10% because the advances in medical technology expected throughout this century will likely occur after you're much older, when the benefits of anticipated new biomedical interventions tend to fade.

So, the short answer is no – it's safe to assume you probably won't make it to 100. You also shouldn't plan on throwing a javelin further than 300 feet or pole vaulting higher than 18 feet. These world records for athletic events that are experienced by just one person are equivalent to the world record for longevity experienced by Jeanne Calment. Just because one person can run that fast, jump that high, or live that long, does not mean we can all accomplish this feat. The vast genetic and lifestyle differences between us preclude this from happening.

When my son Ricky was 10 years old, he wanted to dunk a basketball like his favorite NBA players, and couldn't figure out why he couldn't just make his legs jump higher. When I was in my 30's I tried something similar using the same line of reasoning – I tried running a 4-minute mile after convincing myself that all I needed to do was make my legs move faster. It's a mind/body thing I surmised – all I needed to do was have my mind tell my body what to do.

It didn't work. Try as we might, these feats could not be accomplished because we were both held back by the body design we inherited from our ancestors. That's right, we're blaming our athletic failures on our parents and grandparents! The same holds true for longevity.

But the extreme case of exceptional longevity of Jeanne Calment is interesting for other reasons. When Calment was age 94, her notary made an offer to buy her apartment under the French *en viager* system. This is when a buyer agrees to make regular payments on a property that the seller continues to live in for free while they're alive, in exchange for ownership of the apartment by the buyer when the seller dies. Under most conditions this tends to be a good investment because the seller often dies before enough payments are made to equal or exceed the value of the property.

In this case the Calment apartment deal proved otherwise because the notary had no information on how long Jeanne was going to live. If he had nothing more than access to information on the longevity of Calment's ancestors, he would have realized that she was likely to be long-lived. The average duration of life of her ancestors dating back hundreds of years was in the 70s during a time when life expectancy in France was in the 30s. By the time the notary died, in 1995, he'd spent nearly two hundred thousand dollars, more than twice the value of the apartment, without ever taking occupancy.

When Calment approached her hundredth year, she was still riding her bicycle; and she smoked cigarettes until the age of 115. Near her 100th birthday, Calment went to see the mayor of Arles – the town she lived in. Calment waited patiently in the waiting room outside of the mayor's office, and at some point, the mayor popped his head out to see if

Calment was there and left – declaring that there were no centenarians in the room. She was in fact standing right in front of the mayor wearing a gray suit and a hat with a veil, heeled shoes and seamed stockings – quite elegant apparently.

Calment didn't have the "look of a centenarian" that the mayor was expecting – apparently, she looked at least 20 years younger than her age at the time. This observation is quite common – the children of centenarians all apparently look much younger for their age; probably because they're aging at a slower rate relative to the rest of the population.[1]

The presence of Jeanne Calment is a reminder of what an extreme longevity outlier looks like, but the chances are extremely remote that anyone reading this will live that long. It shouldn't matter though, because enough people are now living well into their 80s and 90s, and some even to 100, to warrant a fresh look at how we deal with retirement planning in the modern era.

---

[1] https://www.newyorker.com/magazine/2020/02/17/was-jeanne-calment-the-oldest-person-who-ever-lived-or-a-fraud

Chapter 5. Gender and Longevity: Are Women "Programmed" to Live Longer Than Men?

Steven Austad

Everyone seems to realize that women live longer than men. For instance, life expectancy at birth for females in the U.S. in 2017 was 81.4 years. For males, it was 76.3 years. The sex difference in longevity at birth is about 5 years. Among ethnic groups, the numbers are similar. Self-identified Hispanic-Americans live about 3 years longer on average than Caucasian-Americans, but the life expectancy difference between the sexes is also about 5 years. In non-Hispanic black Americans, the sex gap in life expectancy is slightly larger – about 6.5 years.

In the 1960's through most of the 1980's the overall American sex difference in longevity was more than 7 years, so someone might surmise that because the difference seems to be shrinking, it might continue to shrink or even disappear in the future. That is unlikely, as the female longevity advantage is one of the most robust features of human biology that we know.

We find it in long-lived countries and in short-lived countries. We find it in the past as well as the present. We even find the same gender advantage in many other species. The difference may shrink or swell a bit over the decades, but it is always there.

In Japan, the longest-lived country in the world, the difference seems to be growing slightly. In the 1960's to 1980's Japanese women lived on average 5-6 years longer than men, more recently that difference has been 6-7 years.

A striking example of the robustness of the longevity gap between the sexes can be seen in the history of Iceland, a country that has tracked its births and deaths assiduously since the middle of the 19th century. In the 180 years from 1840 to the present, Icelandic life expectancy at birth has dipped as low as 18 during famines and disease epidemics and risen as high as today's 82 years, but in every single year over that time, women lived longer than men. A similar pattern can be found in every country and every historical period for which reliable birth and death records exist.

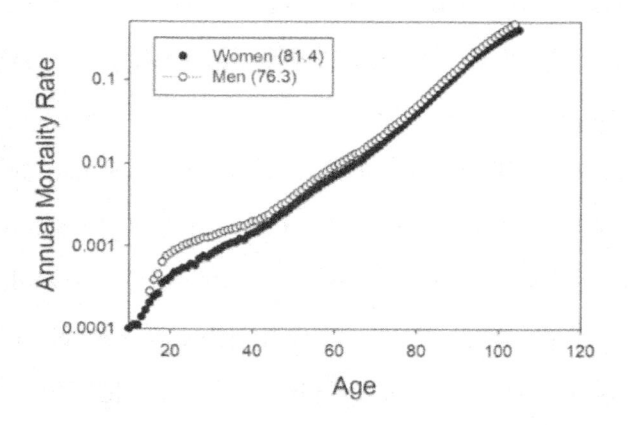

Figure 3. Age-specific mortality rate for women and men in the United States in 2017. Note that after age 40, the increase is linear for both sexes – following the Gompertz law – but the lines are parallel. Males die at a slightly higher, but very consistent, rate throughout life. Numbers in parentheses are life expectancy at birth.
Source: Human Mortality Database (www.mortality.org).

Given this robustness in the longevity advantage of females, a reasonable question to ask is whether women live longer because they age more slowly than men? In the modern world most people die for reasons related to aging. Here the Gompertz law, described in Chapter 1, is informative. Aging rate is often quantified as the rate of increase in mortality rate with age – the slope of the Gompertz line, in other words (Figure 3). As can be seen in the figure, after age 40 when people begin to die for reasons mainly due to aging rather than accidents, men and women's mortality rates increase in almost perfect synchrony. Men and women clearly age at similar rates, men are just slightly more likely to die at any age throughout life.

It is difficult not to conclude that women are better designed for survival than men. After all, women survive better than men before puberty, during their childbearing years, and into old age. Female babies – for reasons we do not yet understand – survive better than male babies. For very prematurely born babies, being male is considered a risk factor for death. Women also survive better in extreme conditions such as famine and epidemics.

This universal female longevity advantage is not due to special resistance to a single disease or cause of death. In the United States currently, after statistically controlling for age, women die at lower rates than men for virtually all the top causes of death with one notable exception. For the "big two," heart disease and cancer which together account for almost half of all deaths, men die at a 60% and 40% higher rate, respectively. For stroke, the sexes die at approximately an equal rate. But Alzheimer's disease is unique in that women die of it more commonly than men. Because the 40% greater frequency of deaths from Alzheimer's disease is adjusted for age, this difference is not due to women's longer lives. Total female deaths from Alzheimer's disease was more than double (actually 2.3 times) that of men in 2016, the latest year for which data are available [Xu, J., et al., 2018. *Deaths: Final Data for 2016. Natl Vital Stat Rep. 67, 1-76*]. The pattern of dramatically greater female deaths from Alzheimer's disease is found not only in the United States but around the world [Austad, S.N., Bartke, A., 2015. *Sex Differences in Longevity and in Responses to Anti-Aging Interventions: A Mini-Review. Gerontology. 62, 40-6*].

Women's predisposition to die at higher rates than men from Alzheimer's disease is significant because the number of people suffering from Alzheimer's is increasing rapidly as the global population ages. As the population continues to live even longer in the coming decades and as the age distribution shifts upward, Alzheimer's disease will have an increasingly more devastating cost both in terms of personal misery and healthcare dollars. The Alzheimer's Association calculates that the current cost of Alzheimer's care and treatment in the U.S. is nearly $300 billion today and they expect that to grow to more than $1 trillion by 2050.

As robust and widespread as is women's survival advantage over men, equally robust, widespread, and more than a little puzzling, is men's health advantage over women in later life. Although women live longer than men everywhere, women in later life also routinely display greater overall rates of physical illness and functional limitations than men. In the United States to take one example, women make more doctor visits, spend more days in the hospital, miss more days of work due to illness, and take more medications than men. Women also self-report more difficulties performing common tasks, more chronic pain, and are overrepresented relative to their proportion of the population in residential care facilities. This is known as the health-survival paradox. It is a world-wide phenomenon, not confined to the United States or western, technological societies.

In self-reported health surveys of people over 50 years old from 13 countries (United States, United Kingdom, 11 continental European countries), it has been demonstrated that despite more men than women being overweight and current smokers, women in all countries were more likely to have disabling conditions. Similarly, consistent differences were found in a comparative study of the United States, Jamaica, Malaysia, and Bangladesh, in which participants were asked about their ability to perform a variety of tasks, such as walk a certain distance, bend over, or climb stairs.

Thus, women live more years than men, but they also live more years in poor health.

The health-survival paradox is likely due to some combination of biological and sociocultural differences. Differences in medical visits and medication use may well be because women are more sensitive to physical discomfort than men and therefore more likely to seek medical attention. However, the fact that men die at higher rates throughout life may also mean that those who survive to older ages may represent a particularly robust subset of all men. Evidence supporting this latter hypothesis can be seen in patterns of mortality during the Covid-19 pandemic. Consistent with virtually all other diseases including other infectious diseases, men are dying of Covid-19 at a higher overall rate than women. However, as we look at older and older victims of the disease, the ratio of deaths between men and women changes.

At ages 55-64, per capita mortality is 87% higher for men compared with women. But as fewer and fewer men remain alive at later ages, that pattern changes. For those 65-74 years old, per capita mortality is 50% higher for men. At 75-84 years when only 75% as many men as women are still alive, the sexes die of Covid-19 at equal rates, and for those over 85 and over, women die at twice the rate of men. The men who survive to these later ages appear to be more robust on average than women who survive to the same ages.

One consequence of women's greater survival throughout life is that the ratio of men to woman decreases with age. About 105 boys are born for every 100 girls. By age 30, there are just about the same number of women and men still alive. By age 70, only about 88 men survive for every 100 women; by age 90 there are 54 men per 100 women, and by the time both sexes hit the century mark only 23 men remain per 100 women.

These changes no doubt have interesting sociological consequences. For instance, according to the Assisted Living Federation of America (ALFA), assisted living communities have a 7:1 ratio of women to men. When combined with the health-survival paradox, the total cost of healthcare for women in later life is likely to become increasingly greater than for men.

Chapter 6. Lifespan Differences Between Spouses Should Drive Investment Strategies: A Case Study

S. Jay Olshansky

In the previous chapter you learned that differences in expected duration of life between men and women are baked into our biology. These differences exist at all ages and across all nationalities, and the fact that something similar occurs in other sexually reproducing species suggests that females are "built to last" better than their male counterparts. However, it is important to avoid interpreting this to mean that among men and women the same age, all of the women will outlive all of the men. To the contrary, this will only be true some of the time.

If you then add in the differences in chronological age between spouses and the inherited and acquired risk factors for health and longevity that couples have or acquire during the course of their lives, you have a recipe for potentially vast differences in survival potential that extend well beyond the generic gender differences in longevity that Steve talked about.

This is particularly important to remember when advising couples on how to plan for their financial future. In fact, evaluating the relative expected lifespan and healthspan of male/female couples and developing a customized financial plan based on this observation, is at the heart of how a Positive Wealthspan is accomplished. Let's dive a bit deeper.

Steve's assessment is of course true at the population level. On average, women outlive men born in the same year beginning at birth, and this longevity advantage lasts into advanced ages. But couples or partners are rarely the same age when they get married, and even if born in the same year, this is no guarantee that the wife will outlive the husband.

In the United States, marriage patterns are such that men tend to be 2.2 years older than their brides at time of marriage – with considerable variation of course. This means that for couples that get married in their 20s, the wife can expect to live about 6.8 years longer than her husband (4.6 years that is baked in biologically at this age plus the 2.2-year difference in their ages when they get married). This difference in survival diminishes somewhat as they age, but not by much. By the time this same couple reaches their mid-60s, the wife can expect to live 4.8 years longer than her husband (2.6-year difference baked into their biology plus the 2.2-year differences in their ages).

If this was the only information used to assess differences in survival between married or partnered couples, this would represent a Stage II longevity assessment. While better than no assessment at all (Stage I), it is still extremely crude and completely void of anything unique about the couple that could generate further separation in survival.

Even subtle differences between spouses have a profound influence on longevity differences between them. For example, one spouse might smoke while the other does not; one may be obese while the other carries a healthy weight; and there may be variation in their levels of physical activity or sleep patterns. Critically important are likely differences in their family history or genetic and acquired differences in disease propensity and/or survival that creates further separation (or no separation at all) between spouses.

Unless these inherited and acquired traits for longevity and health are assessed for couples/partner dyads, a financial planner is left to either ignore these differences entirely (which is the status quo today for many financial planners); rely on generic information based on population level statistics; or choose the same extremely high lifespan estimate (e.g., planning for survival to ages 90-95) as a "safe assumption" to ensure assets are protected for the duration of a hypothetically very long life.

The third option is commonly used today as part of a "sophisticated" computerized Monte Carlo simulation that spreads projected assets out over a lifetime. While it's "safe" in that it overestimates survival for almost everyone, this type of assumption places an undue burden on couples to plan for a survival outcome that is unrealistic for most.

The fact is, sometimes the wife will outlive her husband by decades rather than years; and sometimes the husband will outlive his wife by years or decades. Financial planners and their clients have no way to assess this unless they explicitly open the door to a science-based survival estimate. As you will see, this type of assessment process is neither complicated nor time consuming. *This element of financial planning hinges on science-based assessments of survival for couples, and it is perhaps the best example why Stage III technologies are so desperately needed in financial services today.*

A Case Study

There is no better way to appreciate the value in and importance of couples/partner dyad survival and health estimates for financial planning than to consider a concrete example. The example I'm going to use is a couple that have been close friends of our family for decades. I've changed their names and some details to protect their identity.

The husband – Don – is a 65.4-year-old highly educated professional that is still employed full time at the same job he's had for the last several decades. The wife – Susan – is a 63.2-year-old highly educated professional that is also still gainfully employed full time. Neither has retirement as part of their vocabulary yet, but they're acutely aware that such a time is approaching. Don was approached by a local financial planning professional and was told that now would be a good time to begin preparations for retirement – even if the event itself is several years off. Good advice.

The financial planner used a Stage II longevity assessment approach (he opened up a book with a generic life table in it) and combined that with a fancy sounding Monte Carlo simulation. His conclusion was that both should use age 95 as their targeted lifespan. This was considered a "safe" assumption given that only 25 percent of the men Don's age survive that long.

It was recommended that Don begin taking his social security at age 69, and that Susan could begin as early as age 66. Several investment options were presented, and Don and

Susan gave the idea some thought and then proceeded with their lives – uninfluenced (and apparently unimpressed) by the simple recommendations made by the financial planner.

I spoke with Don and Susan sometime after this assessment occurred and asked if they were interested in a scientific assessment of their lifespan and healthspan in accordance with methods that my colleagues and I have been working on for decades. They agreed.

I first used their exact dates of birth to calculate the baked in biological differences in longevity between them. Given that Don was 2.2 years older than Susan, and generic assessments of survival indicated that Susan would likely outlive Don by 2.3 years, they were already starting out with the likelihood that Susan would outlive Don by about 4.5 years. That in itself would have been far more sophisticated than the simplifying assumption used by the financial planner where both were assumed to survive to age 95. But as it turned out, there was much more to their collective longevity story than I could have possibly imagined.

Susan came into the marriage with a family history of cancer and longevity that rarely exceeded the mid-70s. If one assumes that medical technology will operate more efficiently for Susan than for her ancestors, this could buy her additional survival time; let's say 5 years – a number that is easy to justify using the scientific literature. However, Susan has a history of 20 years of smoking a pack a day; no exercise routine her entire life; excessive alcohol consumption (12+ drinks per week); poor sleep habits; a history of breast cancer; and polypharmacy (she's taking 8 prescribed medications every day for various existing health conditions). Neither parent survived past age 70, and her mother died from breast cancer.

Susan's survival estimate taking all of these factors into account was 73. I'll explain in the next chapter how these personal behavioral risk factors are used to estimate survival.

On top of her survival estimate, the technology Wealthspan has access to allows them to generate for each person an estimate of "healthy life expectancy" [HLE] [also called 'healthspan'] – the number of remaining years of life expected to be in good health. The difference between total lifespan and healthspan is an estimate of the duration of life one should plan to have health challenges and attendant high health care costs. Susan's healthspan came in at 70 with an estimated lifespan of 73.

Don's story is what caught my attention. He comes from a family of exceptionally long-lived individuals – all of whom survived beyond age 90. Both of his parents are still alive (his father is now 102 with all of his activities of daily living intact); his mother is 96. His grandparents survived past age 90 as did his great grandparents and several other members of his extended family.

Don exercises regularly; sleeps 7-8 hours per night; drinks minimal alcohol (2-3 glasses of wine per week); takes no medication and has no diagnosed diseases; and has never smoked. Don and his family show all of the signs of being part of a select group of people known as "super-agers". This is a relatively small subgroup of the population who remain cognitively intact often well past the age of 80, and many retain this high level of mental and physical functioning into their 90s and beyond. While some super-agers often face the same usual health challenges of others after reaching extreme ages, they seem to weather these challenges effectively and bounce back to good health. But there's more.

Don doesn't look a day over the age of 50. Photographs of his father at Don's age found the same phenomenon – he consistently looked 20 years younger than his chronological age throughout his adult life. Even today he maintains the look of a man in his 80s. If you recall, Jeanne Calment from France that lived to 122 also looked young for her age throughout her life. The Mayor of Arles, when peeking his head out of his office door, did not see anyone fitting the description of his vision of what a 100-year-old woman would look like.

This observation about the young face age of extreme elderly individuals is a well-known established phenomenon in aging circles. In fact, we now know that the children of exceptionally long-lived individuals tend to always look young for their age. The reason? Scientists think that these folks look young for their age because, biologically, they are not their age. Biological time seems to be ticking at a slower pace for super agers, which means that someone who is chronologically 100 years old, might in fact face the actual mortality risk of someone that is 20 years younger. With the death rate doubling about every 8 years, this means the actual risk of death for super agers is about one quarter that of the average person their age.

Once I ran Don through my survival analysis, I discovered that his projected lifespan was closer to 95, with a three-fold increase in the probability that he would reach the age of 100 relative to the average man his age in the U.S.

Don and Susan are on totally different survival and health trajectories. None of these nuanced elements to their projected health and longevity were visible to their original financial planner.

Upon further evaluation by a Wealthspan advisor, it was suggested that Susan invest in an asset-based long-term care policy to handle her higher than average chance of facing significant impairments within the next decade. If she didn't need the funds for LTC, those assets would pass on to her surviving relatives. It was further advised that she begin taking Social Security immediately to maximize her income now since her chances of living to her mid-80s was relatively low. While some of her current health challenges are theoretically fixable now, she was not making any effort to do so and seemed uninterested in modifying any of her harmful behavioral risk factors – in spite of being alerted to their impact on her length and quality of life and the benefits of modifying her behavioral risk factors.

By contrast, Don needed to plan for the high probability of surviving to age 100, which meant he should continue working at least into his mid-70s if at all possible. He was further advised to delay receiving Social Security until the maximum age of 70, and that a long-term care policy was ill-advised given the likelihood that he was a descendent of a long line of super agers. It was recommended that a portion of his retirement fund was channeled into an annuity to protect his income stream for what could be a very long life, as well as a whole life insurance policy that could provide a tax efficient income stream at some point down the road and provide a legacy for his children.

By now it should be evident that Stage II and Stage III assessments of health and survival for Don and Susan yield different recommendations. The Stage II assessment fails to take into consideration what is unique (and anything but average) about this couple. *Don is projected to outlive Susan by about 25 years using the Wealthspan assessment tools while the Stage II assessment completely misses the mark on the vastly different life trajectories each member of this couple is on.* Traditional survival models suggesting that the wife will outlive the husband by 4.6 years in this case could lead to a disastrous plan with a high probability of Negative Wealthspan.

The Wealthspan recommendations made sense to Don and Susan because each investment option was directly linked to elements of their lives that they were living at the time. While Susan chose not to modify her lifestyle choices, other couples would hopefully take the opportunity to use the Wealthspan assessment results and make measurable changes to enhance and extend their healthy years of life.

Regardless, Don and Susan are now on a well thought out trajectory to *Positive Wealthspan*, and they both understand exactly why each of their retirement investments is linked directly to attributes of their lives that they can personally see, appreciate, and even modify to their advantage. Their Wealthspan advisor had no difficulty getting Don and Susan to modify their investment portfolio since the tools used to generate their personalized lifespan and healthspan assessments were well justified and easy to understand.

To make life even easier, the assessment by the Wealthspan advisor took less than 20 minutes using his iPad (the assessment could have also been done remotely using a cell phone in the comfort of Don and Susan's home).

Most people are not average. Couples are often on vastly different life and health trajectories. It is just common sense to measure these differences and utilize the tools of science to better inform those seeking advice for retirement planning, and to place into the hands of financial advisors, simple tools and proprietary products that they can feel good about using to help their clients maximize their chances of achieving *Positive Wealthspan*.

III. The Intersection of Wealth Management and Aging Science

Chapter 7. You are not Average! Your Scientifically Determined Lifespan and Healthspan are the Foundation for Your Financial Plan

S. Jay Olshansky

In chapter 6 I provided a real-world example of a couple where the husband had a good chance of surviving to 100 while his wife would probably not live that long. While that was an unusual case, the average lifespan estimates derived from Phase II technologies do not, and should not be applied directly, to most people.

Statistics don't lie here – 95% of the people that share your age and gender, will live either longer or shorter than the averages listed in Phase II generic assessment tables. All of us are as unique as Don and Susan. We each have a personalized longevity trajectory, and that includes both the genetic family history you were born with, the unique environment you were raised in, and the lifestyle choices made during the course of life. Quite simply, most people aren't average!

So, how does an advisor tease out what is different about you, and translate that uniqueness into a personalized assessment of lifespan and healthspan?

Let's begin with lifespan. The traditional way in which a lifespan assessment is made is to examine a mortality table and look up your age and gender; from there you'll see a number that corresponds to the average duration of life for people your age. This estimate of life expectancy (which is called a lifespan for an individual) is based on the observed death rates at your age and above, experienced by the entire U.S. population in the year in which the table applies (usually two years ago). The underlying assumption is that when you reach each age above your own, you'll experience the risk of death of people that age today.

But what if there is something different about you that separates you from others? For example, what if you smoke cigarettes? If I wanted to know how long someone like you might live, I have to depart from the averaging table and calculate how long someone that is a current smoker your age and gender would tend to live. The answer would come from scientific research that documents the life-shortening effect of tobacco use.

I discussed Risk Ratios (RRs) briefly in Chapter 6, so no need for additional detail here, but it's straightforward. Using a male aged 70 as an example, if science tells me that 70-year-old male smokers have a RR of 1.25, this means that the risk of death is 25% higher than the average man this age in the U.S. Now you find out that this person doesn't sleep more than 5 hours; he's divorced; never works out; has a BMI of 38; and his parents died from cancer in their early 70s. Each of those pieces of information separates him from average, and each can be used to adjust his estimate of lifespan. Of course, there are also equally important positive risk factors that are known to extend life.

It's much more complicated than just adding together all of the good and bad longevity attributes possessed by someone. Lifespan calculators are notorious for the use of simple addition and subtraction – these models almost always generate survival estimates that are unrealistically too high or too low. We've solved this problem of additivity by weighting each variable of interest in accordance with first principles of survival analysis. Details are not necessary here, but you should get the idea.

There are more than a dozen primary predictors of longevity that, taken together, yield a highly reliably picture of lifespan that cannot be obtained by ignoring everything that is unique about you. There are plenty more predictors than just 12, but once we discovered that many are correlated with each other, the predictive power of the model did not suffer as we stripped many of them away.

The good news is that your longevity assessment takes only a few minutes, using the smart phone that's already in your pocket or purse. Wealthspan financial advisors have online platforms that perform these lifespan estimates instantaneously – during your meeting with them. The technology that runs this platform was developed by me and a group of research scientists at Lapetus Solutions that also have academic appointments at major Universities in the U.S. and abroad.

How do we know it actually works? That's the easy part, so I'm glad you asked. We conducted a 'back-test' of the technology using the gold standard data set in public health – the National Health and Nutrition Examination Survey (NHANES) that has been tracking the health and longevity of Americans longitudinally for the past 50 years. Just about everything we know in public health about favorable and harmful inherited and acquired risk factors, comes from studies that evaluated data from NHANES.

We applied our predictive model on populations alive in the 1970s and 1980s and tracked who survived and who did not during the last half century. We then examined their personal attributes (including blood chemistry) to see which offered the greatest predictive power. While generating your lifespan estimate will look simple – with no friction involved such as taking blood and urine that is common in insurance underwriting – the science behind this methodology took decades to perfect.

The second estimate provided that is also of great value is called your healthspan or healthy life expectancy (HLE). The science behind this calculation dates back to the late 1970s when scientists realized that the metric of life expectancy was not providing public health professionals with enough information. In public health, we don't just want to know how long someone might live; we also want to know how healthy they are likely to be along the way.

Details of the methodology behind the calculation of healthspan are not important at this point, but the metric itself is extraordinarily valuable in wealth management. Remember Don and Susan? Estimates of healthspan for Don indicated he is likely to experience a very long period of healthy life; to be followed by a compressed period of frailty relative to average. This is common among the children of centenarians. It would be a waste of precious resources for Don to buy a long-term care policy because he's unlikely to need it; but it might make sense for him to invest in what is commonly called an asset-based long-term care policy, which provides LTC coverage if needed, but can be passed along as a death benefit to heirs if long-term care coverage is never required.

By contrast, Susan (his wife) has been making perilous lifestyle choices for many years and is headed down a dangerous path that science has proven often leads to extended periods of frailty and costly medical expenses. While the best choice for Susan would be to change her lifestyle, until she does so, a LTC policy makes sense as part of a retirement strategy to protect their assets.

Without an estimate of healthspan, the advisor is left to guess about LTC recommendations or anything else associated with planning for future health care costs. Advisors armed with these tools provide their clients with a science-based method of estimating healthspan. Advisors love using this technology because he/she can easily explain and justify their investment recommendations; and clients love it because the assessment is quick, non-invasive, and easy to understand. The final decision on what to invest in always rests with the client's comfort level, but the calculation of healthspan offers both client and advisor a simple, fast, and well validated method of finding out what the actual risk is.

A third test that is available through the relationship between Wealthspan and Lapetus is called the Generian Longevity Panel. It's one thing to obtain evidence from self-reported health states about lifespan and healthspan, but science informs us that at a minimum, 25% of survival is influenced by genetic factors. As you get older, this percentage rises significantly as time reveals population subgroups and individuals that won the genetic longevity lottery at birth. If you're over age 50 or 60, genes play a very powerful role in your survival, so measuring this influence is important, possible, and valuable.

The Generian Longevity Panel – developed by scientists at Lapetus – utilizes gene assays collected through 23andMe or other companies that generate similar assessments. This means that if you've already had this genetic test done, all you have to do is download the raw data and submit it to Wealthspan. If you haven't done the test yet, it's very simple – spit into a test tube provided in the 23andMe (www.23andme.com) test kit and place the kit back into the mailbox in its pre-paid packaging. The results come back in about two weeks.

The Generian Longevity Panel report includes information on whether you're a carrier of the two main genetic variants associated with exceptional longevity – and what this means for your personal healthspan and lifespan. Also included is information on whether you're at a higher than normal risk of developing late onset Alzheimer's disease; and your probability of surviving to ages 90+ and 100+ relative to the average person of your age and gender. Frankly, I don't understand how a financial plan can proceed without this information, but I guess most don't know what they're missing until they actually see how it works.

It should be clear by now. You're not average; and the chances that anyone can get reliable information from Stage II generic life assessment technologies is about 5%. With rapid science-based assessments of lifespan and healthspan, wealth management has entered the 21st century of risk assessment. This technology represents a quantum leap for both the wealth managers and their clients, and it should lead to a faster, better, and more customized evaluation process relative to anything being done today.

Chapter 8. Managing Your Investments for the Long-Haul – How to Keep it Simple

Derek Prusa

On January 1, 2008 one of the most famous bets in investment history was made between Warren Buffett (arguably the most successful investor ever) and Protege Partners, LLC (a hedge fund). The bet was simple. Buffett wagered that after all fees, costs, and expenses, an S&P 500 index fund would outperform a predetermined portfolio of hedge funds selected by Protege over the next 10 years, with the end of 2017 serving as the final measurement date. The bet was for $1 million.

Let the time period for this bet sink in for just a moment. Talk about the lousiest timing you could ever imagine for Buffett to bet that a large-cap U.S. stock index would outperform a group of hedge funds (who have the ability to use complex strategies in an attempt to time the market and reduce downside risk). Immediately after the wager started, global stocks plummeted with the 2008 financial crisis. The S&P 500 lost 37% in 2008 alone and was down about 50% at one point in early 2009. Comparatively, the hedge fund portfolio was down only 24% in 2008, so Buffett started in a deep hole.

Following 2008, U.S. stocks went on a wild upward ride while many hedge funds were scared to jump back in. Though maintaining a defensive position did mitigate some of the initial downside loss, the fear of more potential losses resulted in these funds missing almost all of the upside. The S&P 500 outperformed the basket of hedge funds every year after 2008, outside of a 0.3% underperformance in 2015.

Protege conceded the bet early in 2017 as it was evident there was no chance of winning. When 2017 was over, the data showed the S&P 500 gained about 99% total return (7.1% per year) – in spite of the disastrous first year – while the hedge fund portfolio gained just 24% total (about 2.2% per year). It wasn't even close. If the bet didn't start right as we were entering one of the most severe bear markets in history, the difference in returns would likely have been even more staggering.

Buffett was declared the winner, and the proceeds (which totaled $2.2M after the original pot had been invested and grew) went to a charity. While it was all in good fun and benefited a good cause, a very important point had been made.

Promises made by many investment managers that are based on complex strategies – just like Protege Partners did in this wager – are like babies: easy to make, but hard to deliver. The worst part is, by the time you figure out that a complex strategy doesn't work, it's often too late to fix it. You're stuck with a losing strategy for years and your portfolio is already sunk, likely to never fully recover.

So, what is a good rule of thumb to follow when managing investments for the long-haul? The answer comes from a straightforward admonition – ***keep it simple***.

Everyone wants to know how to pick the best investments. Sadly, in a world littered with bad investment advice, it is easier than ever to find the wrong answers. Everywhere you look, firms are touting their "market-beating" strategies – some examples include tactical management, managed volatility, market neutral, arbitrage, and the list goes on. The impression often given is that the more complex the strategy, the better it is. Yet, history has shown us time and time again, when investment strategies are difficult to understand and have too many moving parts, they are almost always destined for failure.

Take Long-Term Capital Management (LTCM) for example. LTCM was a wildly successful hedge fund founded in 1994, led by Nobel-prize winning economists and high-profile Wall Street traders. By 1998, the fund had raised almost $5 billion in assets with the help of stellar market-beating returns. After fees, which were hefty, LTCM returned to its clients 21% in 1995, 43% in 1996, and 41% in 1997. To achieve these returns, LTCM was using an arbitrage strategy to take advantage of temporary price divergences with relatively "low" levels of risk (sounds almost too good to be true, and *complicated*).

With an all-star team running the show and the numbers to back it up, eligible investors were throwing their money at LTCM to manage for them. However, it all came crashing down in 1998. To achieve these huge returns, LTCM was actually highly leveraged, substantially increasing the risk of its positions. Though the fund had just shy of $5 billion in assets, the value of the positions it held was north of $1 trillion, with a significant position in Russian government bonds. In August 1998, Russia defaulted on its debt, creating a liquidity crunch and domino effect that caused the fund to lose nearly all of its assets by the end of September of the same year. This was essentially the end of LTCM; a historic fall after a meteoric rise.

There are plenty of other stories and examples with similar endings to that of LTCM (F-Squared is another interesting case, and for a more current ongoing example check out SoftBank's recent performance, but for the sake of brevity we will leave you to Google these on your own). While not all of the gains and losses are as severe as LTCM, the theme is the same. Investment firms make huge promises, and in some cases are able to provide results for a period of time. But eventually the markets find a way to throw an unexpected curveball and the complex strategies are seen for what they really are – unsustainable.

Beyond the inherently unreliable, complex nature of many of these investment strategies (and trust me, there are a lot), there is another red flag that often gets overlooked: trades and taxes. Generally speaking, tactical, complicated trading strategies place a higher number of trades in client accounts (e.g., there is a lot of movement of funds around to illustrate that they're earning their commissions by "doing something"). While not all trading in portfolios is bad (when used in moderation it can be beneficial), these strategies tend to go above and beyond what is healthy. Their intent is to impress you that they are smarter than the markets, but in the end, this may be little more than an apparent justification for their relatively high management fees. This can result in a negative impact on returns due to higher tax liability (for non-qualified taxable accounts). On top of not really understanding exactly how your money is being managed, you are paying more in taxes! High trading volume and greater complexity are lose-lose scenarios.

Let's look at a simplified example to put some numbers to it. Between 1990 - 2019, the S&P 500 Index (a widely followed large-cap U.S. stock Index) averaged a 9.96% annual return. Assuming you make $80,000 as a married filing joint household, your marginal tax bracket would be 22% (remember tax rates are historically low right now, so this could very well be higher in the future). If you put your money in a tactical investment strategy with a 100% annualized turnover, meaning everything in your portfolio was replaced exactly once, you would need to achieve an average return of over 12.77% to beat the S&P 500.

While 2.81% outperformance may seem plausible on the surface, it is important to note the Morningstar U.S. Large Blend Fund category experienced an average return of just 8.52% over the same time period of 1990 - 2019. This means the aggregate of comparable, professionally managed large-cap U.S. stock Funds actually *underperformed* the Index by

1.44%, and that is before any negative tax implications are accounted for!

Diving further into the drag that taxes can have on your portfolio; assume you have two hypothetical portfolio options: Portfolio A and Portfolio B. Both of these portfolios started in 1990 and were able to buck the trend of underperformance, achieving the same return as the S&P 500, which is 9.96%. While the reported return is the same, Portfolio A experienced only a 15% average turnover and Portfolio B experienced a 100% average turnover. Additionally, Portfolio A was taxed at the more favorable 15% long-term capital gains tax rate while Portfolio B was split 50/50 between long-term capital gains and a higher short-term capital gains tax rate of 22%.

A simple analysis reveals that Portfolio A would have averaged an after-tax return of 9.74% while Portfolio B would have averaged an after-tax return of 8.12%. *This 1.62% better performance for Portfolio A occurred with identical rates of return!* Now a 1.62% difference in any given year won't make or break a portfolio, but compounded over 30 years from 1990 - 2019, this has a HUGE impact. If both portfolios started with $100,000, 30 years later Portfolio A would be worth $1,623,536 while Portfolio B would be worth just

$1,039,604 - a difference of a whopping $583,932. That difference is 5.8 times the original starting value!

So, the "market-beating strategies" these firms are touting are usually complex, not sustainable, and tax-inefficient. And don't even get me started on the higher level of fees these firms typically charge because they're giving clients the impression that they're always doing something with your money – justifying their higher fees. When you cut through the fluff, you find these market-beating strategies are actually just the opposite. They are really setting you up for a higher probability of failure in the long run!

Now, this doesn't mean you can just choose any old indexed ETF and you will be ok. There is still a lot of thought that needs to go into a "simplified" portfolio. The list of investment choices is endless and seems to grow larger every day. And you can't just set and forget your portfolio once you have it up and running either. There are still items that need to be tended to, such as monitoring target bands and managing strategic rebalancing in a tax-efficient manner, but certainly not to the extent seen in more complex funds with lots of costly moving parts.

Furthermore, you will need to find a portfolio that is appropriate for the phase of life you are in and your personal attributes such as lifespan and healthspan estimates through Wealthspan technology that will serve as the fundamental driver of your science-based personalized plan. This is typically best done by working with a Wealthspan professional that is already trained in how to assess your personal needs and desires.

Think of the Wealthspan approach as like going to your doctor. When you get sick, you can search your symptoms on WebMD, find recommendations on how to cure your symptoms, and you will eventually find a solution that is best for you. But the smartest thing you can do, to begin with, is going to the doctor, have an expert review your symptoms, and follow their advice.

While there are different phases of the life cycle, we are going to focus here specifically on the preservation and distribution phases. These parts of the cycle typically start later in your working career and carry into retirement. At this point in life, you are less concerned about achieving the highest possible return in your portfolio, and more focused on achieving steadier cash flow and returns so your portfolio can support your lifestyle throughout the remainder of your lifespan (we will focus on why this is extremely important a little later in the chapter).

Diversifying your investments is important, especially when you enter more mature phases of your life. However, the point of diversification often gets lost as the conversation has become trivialized over the years. Why do we need to diversify? Why can't we just select any old indexed ETF and be ok?

The answer lies in the varying distribution of returns among different asset classes (different types of investments). Nothing works 100% of the time – not a single asset class. Regardless of what you are looking at, individual investments have cyclical ups and downs. This is why it is so important to diversify and include different holdings in your portfolio – to reduce the fluctuations in your portfolio for a smoother, more predictable experience. The older you get, the less volatility you want to see in your portfolio because you're now more interested in maintaining a steady cash flow and more stable rates of return. At a younger age you have the ability to take more risks and still have time to recover if markets turn south, but that isn't the case anymore when you reach the more mature years of your life.

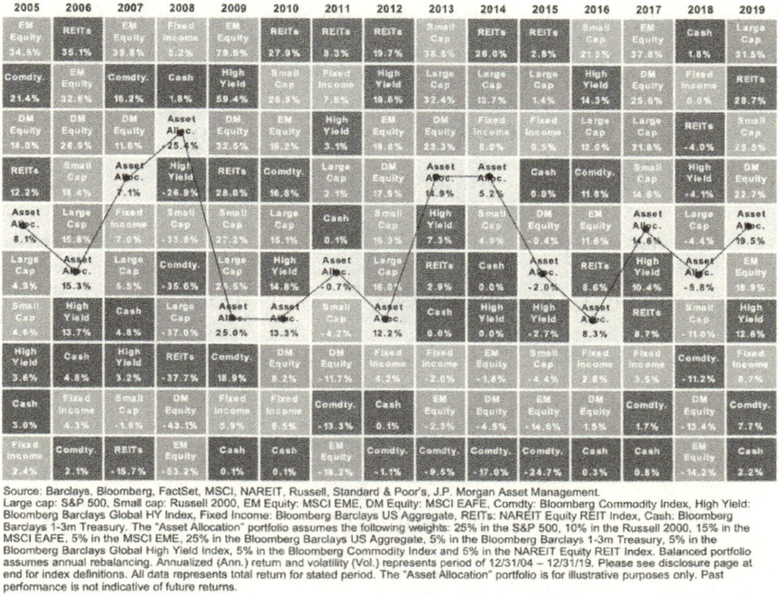

2005	2006	2007	2008	2009	2010	2011	2012	2013	2014	2015	2016	2017	2018	2019
EM Equity 34.5%	REITs 35.1%	EM Equity 39.8%	Fixed Income 5.2%	EM Equity 79.0%	REITs 27.9%	REITs 8.3%	REITs 19.7%	Small Cap 38.8%	REITs 28.0%	REITs 2.8%	Small Cap 21.3%	EM Equity 37.8%	Cash 1.8%	Large Cap 31.5%
Comdty. 21.4%	EM Equity 32.6%	Comdty. 16.2%	Cash 1.8%	High Yield 59.4%	Small Cap 26.9%	Fixed Income 7.8%	High Yield 19.6%	Large Cap 32.4%	Large Cap 13.7%	Large Cap 1.4%	High Yield 14.3%	DM Equity 25.6%	Fixed Income 0.0%	REITs 28.7%
DM Equity 16.5%	DM Equity 26.9%	DM Equity 11.6%	Asset Alloc. -25.4%	DM Equity 32.5%	EM Equity 19.2%	High Yield 3.1%	EM Equity 18.6%	DM Equity 23.3%	Fixed Income 6.0%	Fixed Income 0.5%	Large Cap 12.0%	Large Cap 21.8%	REITs -4.0%	Small Cap 25.5%
REITs 12.2%	Small Cap 18.4%	Asset Alloc. 7.1%	High Yield -26.9%	REITs 28.0%	Comdty. 16.8%	Large Cap 2.1%	DM Equity 17.9%	Asset Alloc. 14.9%	Asset Alloc. 5.2%	Cash 0.0%	Comdty. 11.8%	Small Cap 14.6%	High Yield -4.1%	DM Equity 22.7%
Asset Alloc. 8.1%	Large Cap 15.8%	Fixed Income 7.0%	Small Cap -33.8%	Small Cap 27.2%	Large Cap 15.1%	Cash 0.1%	Small Cap 16.3%	High Yield 7.3%	Small Cap 4.9%	DM Equity -0.4%	EM Equity 11.6%	Asset Alloc. 14.6%	Large Cap -4.4%	Asset Alloc. 19.5%
Large Cap 4.9%	Asset Alloc. 15.3%	Large Cap 5.5%	Comdty. -35.6%	Large Cap 26.5%	High Yield 14.8%	Asset Alloc. -0.7%	Large Cap 16.0%	REITs 2.9%	Cash 0.0%	Asset Alloc. -2.0%	REITs 8.6%	High Yield 10.4%	Asset Alloc. -5.8%	EM Equity 18.9%
Small Cap 4.6%	High Yield 13.7%	Cash 4.8%	Large Cap -37.0%	Asset Alloc. 25.0%	Asset Alloc. 13.3%	Small Cap -4.2%	Asset Alloc. 12.2%	Cash 0.0%	High Yield 0.0%	High Yield -2.7%	Asset Alloc. 8.3%	REITs 8.7%	Small Cap -11.0%	High Yield 12.6%
High Yield 3.6%	Cash 4.8%	High Yield 3.2%	REITs -37.7%	Comdty. 18.9%	DM Equity 8.2%	DM Equity -11.7%	Fixed Income 4.2%	Fixed Income -2.0%	EM Equity -1.8%	Small Cap -4.4%	Fixed Income 2.6%	Fixed Income 3.5%	Comdty. -11.2%	Fixed Income 8.7%
Cash 3.0%	Fixed Income 4.3%	Small Cap -1.6%	DM Equity -43.1%	Fixed Income 5.9%	Fixed Income 6.5%	Comdty. -13.3%	Cash 0.1%	EM Equity -2.3%	DM Equity -4.5%	EM Equity -14.6%	DM Equity 1.5%	Comdty. 1.7%	DM Equity -13.4%	Comdty. 7.7%
Fixed Income 2.4%	Comdty. 2.1%	REITs -15.7%	EM Equity -53.2%	Cash 0.1%	Cash 0.1%	EM Equity -18.2%	Comdty. -1.1%	Comdty. -9.5%	Comdty. -17.0%	Comdty. -24.7%	Cash 0.3%	Cash 0.8%	EM Equity -14.2%	Cash 2.2%

Source: Barclays, Bloomberg, FactSet, MSCI, NAREIT, Russell, Standard & Poor's, J.P. Morgan Asset Management.
Large cap: S&P 500, Small cap: Russell 2000, EM Equity: MSCI EME, DM Equity: MSCI EAFE, Comdty: Bloomberg Commodity Index, High Yield: Bloomberg Barclays Global HY Index, Fixed Income: Bloomberg Barclays US Aggregate, REITs: NAREIT Equity REIT Index, Cash: Bloomberg Barclays 1-3m Treasury. The "Asset Allocation" portfolio assumes the following weights: 25% in the S&P 500, 10% in the Russell 2000, 15% in the MSCI EAFE, 5% in the MSCI EME, 25% in the Bloomberg Barclays US Aggregate, 5% in the Bloomberg Barclays 1-3m Treasury, 5% in the Bloomberg Barclays Global High Yield Index, 5% in the Bloomberg Commodity Index and 5% in the NAREIT Equity REIT Index. Balanced portfolio assumes annual rebalancing. Annualized (Ann.) return and volatility (Vol.) represents period of 12/31/04 – 12/31/19. Please see disclosure page at end for index definitions. All data represents total return for stated period. The "Asset Allocation" portfolio is for illustrative purposes only. Past performance is not indicative of future returns.

Figure 4. JP Morgan Asset Class Performance Chart

Consider the above chart as a way to illustrate this point. While there are many versions of this chart, all including a different mix of asset classes, the goal is to compare individual asset class returns over time.

Each asset class has its moments of outperformance and underperformance relative to the others. Just look at emerging markets! In the bull market from 2003 - 2007, emerging market stocks were among the top three asset classes every time – everyone should have been heavily invested in emerging markets at that time. However, following the 2008 financial crisis, markets shifted as emerging markets found itself in the bottom half more often than the top half over the next 12 years. So, holding too much of this asset class for too long would have caused a major drag on returns.

Another great example is looking at growth vs value styles of investing. From 2000 - 2007, the S&P 500 Value Index outperformed the S&P 500 Growth Index in every year except for one. However, starting in 2008, growth outperformed value eight out of 12 years, illustrating a major shift in market sentiment.

Don't even look at commodities unless you want to feel sick. Talk about not being able to just select any old indexed ETF and let it ride. Commodities produced portfolio ruining returns between 2010 - 2015 if you held too much exposure or were overweight betting on a reversion to the mean.

Finally, why would an investor ever hold bonds? Most of the time they are showing up near the bottom of the barrel. Aggregate U.S. bonds seem to produce lackluster returns in most years. While this is true on the surface, bonds can be absolute portfolio savers during periods of volatility and uncertainty (i.e., 2000 - 2002, 2008, and 2018). During periods when stocks and other riskier asset classes have their worst returns, traditional bonds are able to buck the trend, performing relatively well.

You can create these charts with any number and blend of asset classes and will find the same thing - markets tend to work in cycles and the best asset classes are often unpredictable year-to-year. Emerging markets are great until they aren't. Bonds are a drag on returns until they aren't.

This is why it is important to have an intelligently balanced simple portfolio, created from a blend of various asset classes, designed to last in the long run. It may not be sexy, but it works.

To illustrate my point, let's look at a moderate risk tolerance 60/40 portfolio and compare it to a fully growth-oriented portfolio. While it is important to include a more diversified blend of asset classes and holdings, to keep things simple and easy to follow we are just going to use a blend of 60% S&P 500 and 40% Aggregate U.S. Bonds, compared to just the S&P 500 for growth only. Adding mixtures of other asset classes will only accentuate the data and revelations to follow, so be sure to seek an investment professional like those at Wealthspan Advisors with experience in building appropriate, diversified portfolios.

First, let's take a look at year-by-year returns for each portfolio option (Table 1). We are going to use data from the turn of the century through the end of 2019 (20 years of data).

In most years (13 of the 20 displayed), a 60/40 portfolio underperforms the S&P 500. Understandably, the return for the S&P 500 is also higher than the 60/40 portfolio over this time frame, which makes sense because the more risk you take the more reward you should expect. So, on the surface, investing in a 100% risky asset portfolio seems like a better option.

	60/40	S&P 500	Excess
2000	-0.99%	-9.10%	8.11%
2001	-3.72%	-11.89%	8.17%
2002	-9.82%	-22.10%	12.29%
2003	18.48%	28.68%	-10.20%
2004	8.30%	10.88%	-2.58%
2005	4.01%	4.91%	-0.91%
2006	11.98%	15.79%	-3.81%
2007	6.22%	5.49%	0.73%
2008	-22.06%	-37.00%	14.93%
2009	18.40%	26.46%	-8.07%
2010	12.13%	15.06%	-2.93%
2011	4.70%	2.11%	2.59%
2012	11.32%	16.00%	-4.69%
2013	17.56%	32.39%	-14.83%
2014	10.51%	13.69%	-3.17%
2015	1.25%	1.38%	-0.14%
2016	8.21%	11.96%	-3.75%
2017	14.37%	21.83%	-7.46%
2018	-2.35%	-4.38%	2.04%
2019	22.19%	31.49%	-9.30%

Table 1. Year-by-year returns for portfolio options.

However, looking further into the data, we begin to uncover some important trends. Most notably are standard deviation and maximum drawdowns. Standard deviation (the amount a portfolio fluctuates) is over 40% lower for the

60/40 portfolio compared to the S&P 500. And the maximum drawdown - the largest peak to trough drop - for a 60/40 portfolio is only 32.54% compared to 50.95% for the S&P 500. This data shows that including bonds as a percentage of the portfolio can have a significant impact on reducing fluctuations and the risk of catastrophic loss.

Now this might not be important for *everybody*, but managing risk is extremely important for people nearing or currently in retirement. Especially when it comes to managing the sequence of returns and taking distributions from a portfolio.

What exactly does this mean? Isn't the goal of a portfolio always to achieve the highest return possible? Shouldn't everybody just put all of their money in risky stocks? Who really cares about managing risk anyways? Well, if you are reading this right now, this answer is likely YOU.

Taking a flyer on a "hot stock" to get a potentially large gain may sound great in theory, but in reality, this is not how proper portfolio management works. Talking about your big winners like Apple and Amazon may be fun at cocktail parties, but managing risk is more fun when it comes to your standard of living and portfolio longevity.

And that is exactly what the "40" piece of your portfolio is for - to manage risk and provide a better result during the preservation and distribution years of your life. It's not exciting talking about bond investments (that is probably a lie - some poor soul somewhere has likely been overly excited about their bonds at some point). However, the bond allocation of your portfolio is arguably more important than the stocks when it counts the most.

To further illustrate this point, let's dive deeper into the 60/40 portfolio compared to the S&P 500 (100% stocks). As you recall, the 60/40 portfolio underperformed in 13 of the 20 years from 2000 - 2019. As expected, the S&P 500 beats the 60/40 portfolio on a total return basis over this time period as well. But what if we start taking distributions into account? To do this, we are going to use the simplified, yet popularized, "4% rule" for withdrawals. The 4% rule essentially states you can take 4% of your initial portfolio value, adjusted for inflation, each year in retirement without an overly large risk of running out of money. Specifically, William Bengen conducted a study in 1994 that concluded a 4% annual withdrawal rate should result in a portfolio lasting at least 30 years before becoming fully depleted.

Let's assume we have two portfolios - one following a 60/40 blend and the other following the S&P 500. We will also use January 1, 2000 as a hypothetical start date; a 20-year time frame; and $1 million as the starting value for these portfolios with a standard 3% inflation rate for expenses. Remember, the S&P 500 was better in the majority of years and had a better total return compared to a 60/40 blend. However, the results are astounding when factoring in distributions.

Over the 20-year period, using the 4% rule, the 60/40 portfolio outpaced the S&P 500 by $575,000; over 50% of the original portfolio value! The 60/40 portfolio would still have a value of about $800,000 compared to just $225,000 for the S&P 500 (and with the current COVID-19 pandemic going on as this is written, the difference in values would be even greater). Essentially, the all-stock portfolio is all but depleted while the 60/40 portfolio still has many years to provide support for living expenses going forward.

According to this chart, both portfolios started with a

$1M from 2000 - 2019

— 60/40   — S&P 500

rough patch (does the 2000 dot-com bubble ring a bell?). While the 60/40 portfolio was able to stabilize relatively well following the initial downturn, the S&P 500 portfolio fell much further and struggled to find its footing.

Just when the portfolios looked like they were getting out of the woods, the 2008 financial crisis sent markets crashing down for the second time in a decade. Again, both portfolios were hit, but the 60/40 fared much better than the S&P 500. Especially starting from a much better spot prior to this second crash, the 60/40 portfolio was able to stabilize while the S&P 500 portfolio faltered.

It is worth emphasizing that from March 2009 through the end of 2019, the S&P 500 Index experienced one of the strongest bull markets in its history. Not only was the duration of this bull market unprecedented (it was the longest ever), but the gains were strong as well. Over this period, the S&P 500 gained a whopping 451%! Comparatively, the 60/40 portfolio gained only 240% - a 211% relative underperformance.

Wait a minute, that can't be right. According to the chart the 60/40 portfolio was able to claw back some of its value from the depths of the financial crisis, but the S&P 500 portfolio's value was actually LOWER in 2019 after an almost 11-year bull market in which it experienced a 451% total return.

It seems almost unbelievable, yet the numbers check out. It appears the S&P 500 portfolio will be in total ruin within just a couple of years. This data shows the long-term strength of a non-sexy, blended 60/40 portfolio - further proof that sometimes less is more and that fewer moving parts can be beneficial in a financial portfolio.

Imagine this. You have worked hard your entire life and are finally ready to retire so you can take some vacations, spend time with the grandchildren, and really enjoy life to the fullest. Coincidentally, your first day of retirement happens to be the biggest new year party of your life as Y2K is rolling in. Life is good. Markets have been on a tear and all of these young tech stocks are bound to continue driving stock prices even higher. There is no end in sight as technology and the world are changing rapidly.

Then *it* happens. The dot-com bubble bursts and markets come crashing down. Things are a little rough for a few years, but in 2003 markets started to rally again. It took a little while to pick up momentum, but by 2007 everything seems to finally be back to normal and markets are back near all-time highs. Real estate is hot and with all of this home buying activity the economy appears to be set to roar into the future.

Then *it* happens, again. The 2008 financial crisis hits and stocks are halved for a second time. This one hurts a little more. It always does the second time around. However, markets start to rebound again in early 2009 and go on a tear. There is a little more caution in the early years this time as doomsayers linger around a bit longer, but more confidence is slowly built each year the markets move higher. Eventually, everybody is all-in again. 2017 is the least volatile year in the history of the S&P 500 and things can't get better. Despite a few minor bumps along the way, we see the longest bull market in history with no end in sight.

Then *it* happens a third time with the Covid-19 pandemic in 2020 (data not included in the analysis as this is still ongoing at the time of writing this).

This story has two completely different endings, depending on the portfolio you selected at the start of your journey.

If you went with the standard S&P 500 stock portfolio like many people, you see the writing on the wall as you are about to run out of assets. All of those vacations and extra gifts for the grandchildren will be a distant memory as you must now significantly rein in your lifestyle just to afford the bare necessities. "The market will eventually rebound, so just hang in there" they said time and again. While this is true from an economic perspective, the Market doesn't consider that you have had to take distributions for the past 20 years. Yes, the S&P 500 Index is well above where it was when you retired, but your portfolio is much much lower.

However, if you went with what we consider to be the more appropriate simple 60/40 portfolio, you are afforded more wiggle room to continue living life as you imagined when you took the plunge 20 years ago.

Now I know what some of you are thinking. "This is an extreme scenario, and what are the odds that this would happen to me? Bad luck with retirement and market timing is something that only happens to other people." We see this all too often as many people have this common "optimism bias", which results in underestimating risks and failing to take proper precautions for their specific situation.

The sad reality is, this scenario did happen to a lot of people and it's not possible to know in advance that it won't happen to you, so planning for this eventuality is part of smart portfolio management. Unfortunately, this ruined a lot of retirements, but the ones who were properly allocated and invested were able to hold up even in the face of disastrous market scenarios.

There is always the potential for another market crash around the corner. Things seem good when markets are moving up and to the right. It happens every time. "Nothing can go wrong. This time it's different." That seems to be exactly when disaster strikes, resulting in portfolio ruin – and we don't like taking those kinds of risks on behalf of our clients.

It should be evident by now – the sequence of returns can have a major impact on your portfolio, especially when you are taking distributions, which is why it is so important to have a properly allocated portfolio that balances both risk and return, and which take into consideration your personalized projected lifespan and healthspan.

While the 60/40 portfolio is by no means perfect - it isn't the magic pill that gets you 10% a year guaranteed returns with no risk - it simply works. It has been tested time and again, and every time it has held up. Even in one of the least favorable periods ever to start taking distributions, the portfolio was able to provide continued stability.

Largely, this can be attributed to the fact that stocks and bonds rarely have negative performance in the same year. Going back to 1928, this has only happened four times (1931, 1941, 1969, and 2018). With at least either stocks or bonds profitable 95% of the time, it greatly reduces the risk for catastrophic losses. In these uncertain times, risk reduction helps our clients maintain the confidence needed to enhance the probability of achieving *Positive Wealthspan*.

Complex, black box, overly tactical strategies have let investors down repeatedly. Every time one fails two more pop up, writing checks they can't cash. The cycle is relentless, and it draws in unknowing investors every time because it sounds good and they want to believe it is true. These investors are willing to give another firm a chance because 'this time it'll be different' and they need to catch up from the mistake they made trusting the last company that failed them.

You have seen the data and you know better. The next time you make an important decision with your life savings, follow the advice of highly successful wealth management advisors like Warren Buffet; stay away from complexity and embrace a Wealthspan-style strategy that is simple, smart, and proven. Maybe the 60/40 portfolio will be recommended, but perhaps something different will be appropriate based on your personal circumstances and projected lifespan and healthspan. Your financial goals, tolerance for risk, and science-based estimates of longevity and health will determine what is best for you. *It's never too early or too late to start investing wisely, so the best time to start is now.*

Chapter 9. Uncovering a Hidden Asset to Increase Wealthspan

Jay Jackson

From the moment we transition into the work force, we should begin thinking about retirement. If we plot and plan correctly and properly calculate the age and exact savings needed to retire with the funds required to maintain our health and happiness well into retirement, the daydream of years and decades in a happy post-retirement phase of life could, and should, become reality. But notions of retirement in this country have changed rapidly in recent years. While some are content with exiting a lifetime of work to enjoy the gift of a long life as have past generations, in the modern era, many people want or need to keep working. Both scenarios require advanced planning. For those late to the planning game, this chapter will inform you about a potentially lucrative financial asset you are likely unaware you have.

As highlighted in this book, thanks to incredible advances in medical science, preventative care and better awareness of healthy living, many Americans are living longer and healthier lives than at any time in our history. While an increasingly larger proportion of our lives can be lived in post-retirement if we choose to do so, the extension of healthy life also means that staying in the labor force longer is possible for some and required for those that failed to plan properly. The challenge now is that for many people, their life-long savings for retirement have not kept up with their anticipated extended lives. This phenomenon of a disconnect between expected longevity and accumulated lifetime savings, if any, has been recognized by AARP as one of the major challenges for older generations in this century - leaving more seniors financially unprepared to enjoy the gift of their longer lifespan.

This gap in retirement savings relative to anticipated longevity has been coupled with a 200 percent rise in bankruptcy rates since 1991 for a rapidly growing cohort of Americans over the age of 65. The result is an unprecedented number of retirement-aged Americans forced to remain in the workforce longer than originally planned – the highest we've seen in almost six decades. This is a legitimate crisis for our aging population.

As someone who talks directly to senior citizens on a daily basis as part of my work, I can personally attest to the magnitude and impact of this crisis. I intend to enter the ranks of retirement someday, but my own pursuit of a financially secure later phase of life in good health (positive

Wealthspan) will be driven by advanced planning. Among those I see today that did not plan well, many are literally and figuratively sick with worry, unable to sleep at night because they don't know how they'll find the money to pay their expenses today or in the future. Their retirement daydreams in their younger days that were filled with visions of activities and travel are often replaced with the very real, very scary scramble to just make ends meet – today. Those approaching retirement right now are part of a huge baby boom cohort that is being forced to find financial solutions *after* they retire. For many, the solution means postponing retirement, sometimes indefinitely, or making serious financial sacrifices to get or stay just north of the poverty line.

A surprisingly simple solution to a more financially secure retirement exists today for many seniors, and my goal here is to make you aware of this option.

Life Insurance is Personal Property and May Be Your Ticket to an Enhanced Wealthspan

After homeownership, life insurance policies, including term life policies, are often the largest financial asset that people acquire during the course of life. Owners of life insurance policies have been doing the right thing their entire lives – making regular payments to the insurance company, protecting their loved ones from unexpected events, and securing the peace of mind that comes with the purchase of life insurance. However, few people realize that their policy actually belongs to them as a tangible and often substantial financial asset – it does not belong to nor is it owned by the insurance company. You own it! More than 90 percent of people do not know they can actually sell their policy while they are alive, or a portion of it, if there is a better use today for the life insurance equity they've accumulated during the course of life.

U.S. Supreme Court Ruling

In 1902, a man by the name of Burchard took out a life insurance policy on his own life, made two premium payments, was late on the third and, needing surgery but having no money to pay for either the surgery or his life insurance, sold it for $100 to the doctor doing his surgery (Dr. Grigsby). Burchard subsequently passed away from causes unlikely to be associated with the surgery. The administrators of the insured's estate sought to recover the insurance payout from its beneficiary, Dr. Grigsby. This led to a legal fight that made its way to the U.S. Supreme Court.

In a landmark 1911 ruling of Grigsby v Russell, with a majority opinion written by Justice Oliver Wendell Holmes, the U.S. Supreme Court (SCOTUS) concluded that "The rule of public policy that forbids the taking out of insurance by one on the life of another in which he has no insurable interest does not apply to the assignment by the insured of a perfectly valid policy to one not having an insurable interest. In this case, [the Supreme Court] *held* that the assignment by the insured of a perfectly valid policy to one not having any insurable interest but who paid a consideration therefor and afterwards paid the premiums thereon was valid, and the assignee was entitled to the proceeds from the insurance company as against the heirs of the deceased."

The simple translation of this court ruling is that the purchasers of insurance policies retain ownership and have the option to sell part or all of that policy to someone else while they are alive. The SCOTUS ruling is fundamental to helping people realize the benefit of an investment they thought would only yield financial benefits after death. Justice Oliver Wendell Holmes, Jr., a keen legal scholar, understood the important relationship between the law and economics.

In his opinion, Holmes wrote, "....life insurance has become in our days one of the best recognized forms of investment and self-compelled saving. So far as reasonable safety permits, it is desirable to give life policies the ordinary characteristics of *__property__*."

Fortunately, Burchard invested in an insurance asset he could sell (one worth almost the equivalent of $2,500 today, adjusted for inflation since 1911) and was therefore able to enhance or prolong his life by being able to pay for his surgery using the proceeds of the sale of his insurance policy. That Supreme Court ruling is particularly relevant today with so many people approaching retirement ages with insufficient funds available to achieve a positive Wealthspan, and it opens the door to a tangible retirement asset that most people carrying life insurance are unaware they own.

Awareness is the key

Over the last few years, the option to sell a life insurance policy has seen a surge of interest as more seniors grapple with an uncertain financial future. In spite of this surge, the vast majority of the public that owns life insurance, and their financial advisors, are still unaware that this tangible asset is available as a method of helping to secure a positive Wealthspan. Selling part or all of a life insurance policy is not the right choice for everyone, but what the retirement savings gap crisis illustrates is that people need a better understanding of the broad range of financial alternatives and options that are currently available to them.

Everyone has the right to know their insurance policy is their property and can choose to do with it what they like. Selling a policy to recoup the current equity can be a far better option than continuing to pay increasingly high premiums or allowing the policy to lapse, which happens to a stunning 99 percent of term life policies.

The effort led by lobbyists who represent the very insurance companies that measured the risk, issued the policy, and profit by the premium stream, are in conflict with the policy holders who would benefit from this financial option. Part of the insurance model is not only a bet on how long the policy holder is likely to live, but an actuarial assumption that a high percentage of policy owners will eventually stop paying the premiums after a given number of years – referred to as a lapsed policy. Policy owners may also have the option of surrendering the policy to the insurance company for an embarrassingly low cash surrender "value", without ever knowing that the insurance policy could be sold in an open market to someone willing to pay considerably more for that policy than the insurance company from which it was originally purchased.

You would not make this mistake with your home or any other tangible financial asset that you own.

Enhancing Wealthspan by Transforming Your Life Insurance Policy into A Retirement Asset

Insurance carriers have tried to enter the space as a buyer of their own policies. One carrier has launched a policy buyback program called "Enhanced Cash Surrender Value" (ECSV). This program is offering their clients a purchase price higher than the current cash surrender value, which by legal definition is referred to as a "life settlement". However, the carrier argued to state insurance regulators they are purchasing their own paper; therefore, proper disclosure and life settlement documentation is not required.

The ECSV program does not follow the definition of fair market value and does not pretend to. It is designed so that the carrier can purchase their risk back from the consumer at a deeply discounted price to the fair market value. There is an obvious potential conflict of interest here that is ripe with potential litigation. The ECSV program, in my view, is designed to enhance the profits of the insurance company first. I'm here to tell you that there is another option that can be far more profitable to owners of insurance policies.

Transaction Benefits

Notwithstanding a well-established, 110-year-old U.S. Supreme Court ruling; efforts by insurance companies to buy back policies; and the rise of the life settlement industry that offers more lucrative returns on this investment, has led to stories of policy owners retaining their quality of life and financial independence by exercising their right to tap into this valuable accumulated lifetime asset. Consider the following example:

> Violet is a 92 years old woman that had outgrown the need for her life insurance policy as her monthly insurance premium cost was increasing every year beyond her means to pay. Violet struggled to make the payments but also wanted to make sure her heirs still received an inheritance. Violet was offered $150K cash for her 750K life insurance policy, plus, she was able to keep a $300K interest in the policy to pass onto her heirs. Violet accomplished exactly what she needed to do – she eliminated her insurance premium payments to improve her monthly cash flow; she had immediate access to a sizeable sum

of money accumulated in her policy that she did not know she could tap into; and she kept her promise to her heirs that they would receive a sizeable inheritance. This decision helped Violet maintain or improve her current standard of living and eliminated the worry and financial hardship associated with paying premiums she could not afford.

There are thousands of stories just like this throughout our industry, and hundreds of thousands more are possible if knowledge of the value of life insurance policies was more well known. Millions are spent each year to acquire policies just like Violet's, but the challenge faced by the life settlement industry is that hundreds of millions of dollars are on the sidelines that could be deployed, but lack of awareness for this transaction means that a large number of people are not benefitting from this option. There simply are not enough policies to purchase to spend the available investment capital. It is a classic example of demand exceeding supply. This means it is a sellers' market right now and will likely remain so for the foreseeable future.

We conducted market research nationwide and determined that less than 1% of people who could benefit from this transaction are aware that it exists. *Policy sellers can be paid an average of 8 times above the policy cash surrender value.* With lapse rates so high and a financial benefit this significant for seniors, it is unfortunate that more people are not taking advantage of this financial opportunity. With increased regulatory oversight and an alignment of institutional capital, this is the perfect storm to increase Wealthspan.

Keep in mind that the proceeds currently received from selling a life insurance policy, when they do occur, are often reinvested into other financial products including long-term care, to cover medical expenses, pay off debt, and also to fund vacation and 2nd homes. Estate planning and gifts to heirs are evolving to include future inheritance enjoyed while the grantors are alive.

There is no shortage of ways to leverage the value of life insurance policies to better plan for a positive Wealthspan. In addition to improved cash flow, there are other benefits to the insured that are less obvious. Prospects for a longer than average lifespan and an extended post-retirement period is a key factor to consider when purchasing a life insurance policy. Buyers of insurance policies adjust the mortality assumptions of the insured to take into consideration the shift in longevity that is likely to occur relative to the averaging assumptions used by the insurance companies. This often benefits the policy owner significantly. The owners of the life insurance policies choose of their own accord to sell their policies, and the added financial security they receive as a result has a material positive affect on their quality of life and peace of mind going forward.

Historical Pay-outs and Process

Let me re-emphasize the fact that sellers are often paid more than 8 times the policy holder's current cash surrender value for their policy. This multiple is likely to remain this favorable for years to come. The market is well capitalized – funded by large institutional capital. The challenge is that the capital significantly outweighs the number of policies available for purchase, so my goal in this chapter, in part, is to inform policy holders that they have a potentially significant asset on hand that can be used to amplify the financial security of their retirement. Informing the wealth management advisors of these policy holders about this asset class is equally important. Based on the current interest rate environment, it is reasonable to assume this asset class will remain a favorable sellers' market for the foreseeable future.

Solving for Net Present Value

The true value of a life insurance policy is estimated using a metric known as Net Present Value (NPV); also known as

Market Value. This measure is the difference between the present value of cash inflows and the present value of cash outflows over a period of time. NPV is used in investment planning to analyze the profitability of a projected investment, so calculating NPV when considering selling a life insurance policy is important.

There are three basic components needed for a seller to know the NPV or Market Value of their life insurance policy:

- Duration (Projected Lifespan of the policy holder)
- Future Cost (Inforce Policy Ledger)
- Assumed Investor Rate of Return

With these three pieces of information, any policy seller can estimate the NPV of their policy. Access to the data points is becoming more readily available to advisors and their clients. Sellers can now quickly receive a policy market valuation to make an informed decision regarding the true value of their life insurance policy.

Historically, the duration was the most challenging piece of information to acquire in the equation, but it is possible for sellers, their advisors, and buyers, to estimate duration in just a matter of minutes. Once you have a clearer picture of your own lifespan, the other two valuation points are simple.

The insurance company will provide a future inforce ledger detailing the future costs of the policy.

It is important that you view your policy with the same approach as an investor when deciding whether you want to sell your policy or keep it. Knowing your estimated lifespan will tell you how you should continue to fund your policy should you choose to keep it. Here's how it works. The insurance company will illustrate your policy with the assumptions of a hypothetical maturity – companies typically assume age 95 or age 100. This ledger will assume that you will want to fund your policy to this estimated maturity, even if your personal chances of living that long are remote. However, if your projected lifespan is lower, say to age 88, and the chances of living to 95 and older is remote, then you would be overfunding your policy by at least 7 years if the higher projected lifespan is used to fund the policy.

The life insurance company only pays the policy death benefit to your heirs; they retain the overfunded cash surrender value. Therefore, you need to only fund your policy with the minimum cost of insurance required to keep the policy inforce. *Yes, your cost of insurance will increase over time but why would you overfund the premiums for the life insurance company to earn interest on?* As an investor we only pay the minimum future premiums because we have an independent and more reliable estimate of duration that comes from the Wealthspan platform. When solving for Net Present Value you need to take this into consideration.

The final component is the assumed investor rate of return or IRR. Historically, the discount rate applied is 10-12%. It has been as high as 18% post 2008 and as low as 8%. Based on the current capital in the market it is reasonable to use 10-12% as a starting point.

How would this formula apply to the example of Violet described earlier? Violet is 92 years old with an average 3.5-year remaining lifespan. The face value of the policy is $750K with annual premiums of $62.5K. Assuming a 10% IRR and her heirs retaining $300K of the policy, Violets NPV is $150K. New technology has made it possible to solve for NPV in minutes after establishing the lifespan.

To break the valuation down a little further:

Face Value = $750,000 - $300,000 Retained for Beneficiary = $450,000
Lifespan - 3.5 years
Premiums to Lifespan = $62,500 x 3 = $187,500
IRR = 10% (rule of 72 using 3.5 years) = $112,500 investor return
NPV = $150,000 ($450K - Investor Return $112,500 - Premiums to Lifespan $187,500)

Summary

Life insurance is personal property and a valuable asset, but it is seldom used that way. It is indisputable that seniors who may be facing financial challenges in retirement or when planning for it, have the right to know about the option to reclaim the equity in their life insurance policy while they're alive. Financial advisors helping their clients with life planning also need to know about this important asset class and the companies available to purchase policies.

As our longevity continues to increase and as 10,000 people per day reach their 65th birthday in the U.S. today, it is vital that the huge baby boom generation become aware of the full value of all of their assets. The fact is that few are even aware that their life insurance policies can be leveraged as a significant asset that has the potential to dramatically improve the chances of achieving a positive Wealthspan.

To summarize, this generation is driven by poor financial planning and a lack of understanding of what's required to enhance their own Wealthspan through the course of life. The first step in curbing the financial concern and uncertainty felt by individuals and families across the country is to start providing the information and options necessary for them to prepare for their own economic future.

Chapter 10. The Importance of a Financial Plan

Ben Webster

We've all heard the term 'financial planning', but what exactly does this mean? How exactly does a financial plan lead to a *Positive Wealthspan*? Here we shed light on the importance of having a holistic financial plan in place and how this plan can help you achieve what Hyman Roth wanted from the start – health and wealth and happiness all woven together; but not just in post-retirement years – throughout life.

Financial planning, by definition, is the process of determining whether and how an individual can meet life goals through proper management of financial resources. Holistic financial planning goes further – encompassing additional details such as tax planning, retirement planning, education planning, estate planning, insurance planning, and investment management. It's important to implement a holistic approach when creating a financial plan as each of these sub-categories are important on their own, but when considered collectively, they allow an advisor to work with you to plan for the big picture. This is especially important as the fiduciary standard becomes the new "gold standard" in advisor-client relationships.

A majority of advisors fall into one of two categories. They are either bound by a 'fiduciary' or a 'suitability' standard. While these may sound similar, they are not governed by the same standards. Per the Investment Advisers Act of 1940, Investment Advisers have an overarching duty to act in their clients' best interests – that is the definition of a fiduciary. On the other hand, investment brokers serve the broker-dealers who they work for and must believe their recommendations are 'suitable' for clients (the suitability standard).

There can be a big difference in something that's suitable for a client versus what is in their best interest. This allows a client to choose between working with an advisor who is required to place their interests ahead of the advisor's interests, or working with a salesperson (a broker), who sells a product that serves the interest of the broker-dealer.

There's no shortage of insurance agents and brokers anxious to sell you and everyone else the next best product, but the client has to ask themselves "how does this fit into my plan, and is this the best solution for me?" This is exactly where a clear distinction is made between working with a fiduciary and a broker-dealer.

Individuals can work with a broker and buy a product, but

has that broker fully educated the client on this product? Do they truly understand the effect this product could have on their overall plan and goals? Is the broker even aware of the current and projected lifespan and healthspan of the client and his/her family? Did the broker even create a financial plan? It's possible, but not likely, because that's not their goal.

In working with a fiduciary and implementing a holistic financial plan, it's important that the advisor educate the client to help them better understand how using proper financial tools and services can increase the probability of success in securing a *Positive Wealthspan*.

Consider the following example. Purchasing through a broker, assume an individual just bought 1,000 shares of a mutual fund, at $10/share, within their taxable (individual) account. The client now owns the mutual fund, but what long-term consequences were considered prior to the purchase and what advice can they expect to receive moving forward?

The client should be asking before the investment is made "What are the future tax implications? Does this align with my current risk tolerance? How does this fit into my overall plan?" These are questions that a fiduciary would ask before the transaction is even considered. By contrast, a broker may be hesitant to answer these questions as it's considered advice and they are not held to the same standards as a fiduciary.

This can make it difficult for the investor to understand what to do moving forward and will likely prompt them to seek additional advice in the future or try their hand at self-managing their assets. Without proper guidance, it's easy to understand how a client could be left in the dark and stuck with an investment that was never the best fit for their unique circumstances to begin with.

Now, let's assume the same investor is working with an advisor who practices as a fiduciary and assists the client in implementing a holistic financial planning strategy that is in their best interest. Studies show that this often results in a better working relationship for the advisor and the client as the advisor can educate the client in advance of the investment and help them better understand how this investment fits into their overall plan.

Continuing with the first example, let's assume the investor held the mutual fund for years and is now nearing the end of their life. The investment is currently valued at $40/share, originally purchased at $10/share. At this point, the client has returned large gains within the mutual fund and doesn't know what to do.

Unless they have a previous investment or financial planning experience, there's a good chance they don't know what's going to be in their best interest. If they were working with a Wealthspan Advisor – all of whom have the designation of fiduciary – this scenario would have already been part of an implemented strategy.

For example, it could make sense for the investor to leave the investment to an heir, we'll assume a daughter in this case. In doing so, the daughter will inherit the mutual fund and receive a step-up in basis to the funds' current value as of the date of death. The market value of the shares on the day the owner dies becomes the daughter's cost basis. The daughter provides the mutual fund company proof of identity along with a death certificate, a probate court order, or other documentation. The company either transfers the shares to an account in the daughter's name or sells the shares and sends the proceeds to her.

If the client was to sell the mutual fund prior to death, they would be responsible for paying long-term capital gain tax on $30,000 in gains, assuming a cost basis of $10,000 and a market value of $40,000 when sold. If the mutual fund is valued at $40/share at the date of death, by leaving the asset to the daughter, the client is able to avoid any tax implications on the gains. The daughter will now have a cost basis of $40,000, avoiding having to pay tax on the $30,000 gain altogether. Assuming the original investor would've been in a 15% long-term capital gains rate, this strategy would equate to a $4,500 savings in taxes ($30,000*0.15).

It's important to understand that the creation of a financial plan is not the same as a collection of arbitrary financial decisions during the course of life. In the previous example, it wasn't by chance that the daughter inherited her father's assets and took advantage of the step-up in cost basis. This would have been the product of a detailed, comprehensive decision, planned for by the daughter and her financial advisor well in advance. It's the advisor's obligation to educate and provide the client with the knowledge and tools to make the best decisions that fit her comfort level.

When creating a financial plan, there's no one right answer because risk tolerance will vary from one person to another. However, at least the science of lifespan and healthspan estimation from Wealthspan Advisors should yield consistently valuable information about an individual that would not otherwise be available. The client has to be comfortable with the decisions they make; otherwise, this can lead to a lack of confidence and inevitably dismantle the plan prior to implementation.

How do individuals ensure their advisor is taking the proper steps to give them that confidence needed for implementation? Luckily, there are 'best practices' advisors can utilize to ensure they're doing just that. The following are practice standards which ultimately provide the advisor with the steps necessary to create and implement a holistic financial plan in hopes of increasing the client's potential for achieving *Positive Wealthspan*;

Understanding an Individual's Personal and Financial Situation

- It's imperative for the advisor to obtain both qualitative and quantitative information.
    - Examples of qualitative information include a client's self-reported health, values, beliefs, attitudes, biases, expectations, human capital, risk tolerance, goals, needs and current course of action, assuming they continue doing what they're currently doing;
    - Examples of quantitative information include a client's age, dependents, salary and income, liabilities, assets, savings, taxes, employee benefits, government benefits, insurance coverage, estate plans, projected lifespan and healthspan, and capacity for risk.

- This step is exceptionally important as it gives the advisor an opportunity to understand the client's situation in its entirety;
- This is an opportunity for the advisor to address any missing information that would be essential in the planning process.

Identifying and Setting Goals

- The definition of financial planning is the process of determining whether and how an individual can meet life goals through the proper management of financial resources. With that being said, identifying and setting goals is a crucial step within the planning process;
- It's the advisor's responsibility to assist the client in setting goals based on the information revealed in the first step of this process. It's important for the client to understand what the effect of one particular goal may have on other goals;
- This is also an opportunity for the advisor to set realistic expectations and assumptions based on the goals set. This includes estimated lifespan and healthspan, future tax rates, risk and return metrics, inflation, inheritances, and other material assumptions.

Analysis of the Client's Current Situation and Identification of Potential Alternatives

- In this step of the evaluation process, an analysis is performed on the client's current situation, resulting

in the likelihood of them being able to meet all their goals assuming they make no changes to their current plan;
- At this time, it's also important to analyze potential alternative courses of action, including the advantages and disadvantages of each alternative, while ensuring relevance to meeting their set goals.

Developing and Presenting the Holistic Financial Planning Recommendations
- Up to this point, the financial professional has assisted in setting goals and ran an analysis on both their current and potential wealth roadmaps – now it's time to develop and present recommendations based on their findings;
- It's important to consider the following information when developing recommendations;
    - The assumptions and estimates used in developing recommendations;
    - What bearing does each recommendation have on other recommendations?
    - Priority and timing.
- The advisor can now present the recommendations to the client, including all of the details considered for the recommendations.
    - It's essential that the client understands how these recommendations facilitate a solution in reference to meeting their established goals.

Implementation of Recommendations

- The advisor and client must mutually agree on the implementation responsibilities of each party;
- The client's essential responsibility is to accept or reject the recommendations set forth by the advisor;
- The advisor's responsibilities may include, but are not limited to:
    - Providing the necessary steps for implementation;
        - For both the client and advisor
    - Referring and coordinating with other professionals;
        - The advisor may recommend the implementation of a trust at which point they refer the client to an estate attorney who will assist them in setting up the proper documentation.
    - Selecting and securing products and/or services;
        - Again, it's vital the advisor is acting in a fiduciary capacity and ensuring the recommendations are in line with the client's goals, needs, and priorities.

Monitoring
- Monitoring a client's situation after the plan is set in motion is a crucial step in the planning process as everyone's lives are in constant flux:
    - It's important that clients meet with their advisors at least annually to ensure they're still on track to meet their goals and needs;

○ We all understand that life happens and individuals need to be prepared to adjust their plan and goals based on their current personal and financial position.

By utilizing practice standards as a guideline for the financial planning engagement, the advisor can ensure they have taken the proper steps to add value for the client, which will in turn assist in solidifying their relationship. Without bringing value to the relationship, it's hard to justify an advisor charging for any services rendered. There must be a correlation between the services provided to the client and how that's going to help them meet their goals.

Over the years, we've seen the financial planning industry change in terms of how advisors add value. In the past, many advisors would pride themselves on their investment management skills, touting an outperformance history relative to benchmarks. In recent years, we've seen the industry skew in the direction of a service-centric model. With that being said, it lends an opportunity for the advisor to separate themselves from the pack based on the services they offer. The additional value-add an advisor brings to the table can be defined as the advisor's "alpha".

Vanguard is a company that understands how the industry has changed and is continuing to evolve over time.

They've conducted research on "alpha" and the additional value advisors can bring to the table. Vanguard defines their advisor's alpha as a "concept that outlines how advisors can add more consistent value, or alpha, through wealth management in the form, for instance, of financial planning, behavioral coaching, and guidance — rather than outperforming a policy portfolio, which has historically been the primary value proposition for many advisors."

While investment management is still a spotlight within the financial planning process, Vanguard understands the value proposition is a lot more than just picking the right investments. "The confusion can grow if the advisor has based his or her value proposition primarily on an ability to deliver better returns for the client, as many do. But better returns relative to what? For many advisors and clients, the answer would be "better than the market," but a more pragmatic answer for both parties might be "better than investors would most likely achieve if they didn't work with a professional advisor." In this framework, an advisor's alpha is more aptly demonstrated by relationship-oriented services that provide discipline and reason to clients rather than trying to beat the market.

As the industry continues to gravitate towards a service-centric model, there is a temptation to define an advisor's value-add as an annualized number. In 2016, Vanguard published a Whitepaper in an attempt to do just that. See Figure 6 below to better understand how Vanguard quantifies the value-add of best practices in wealth management by implementing specific strategies or "modules":

Vanguard Advisor's Alpha strategy	Module	Typical value added for client (basis points)
Suitable asset allocation using broadly diversified funds/ETFs	I	> 0 bps*
Cost-effective implementation (expense ratios)	II	40 bps
Rebalancing	III	35 bps
Behavioral coaching	IV	150 bps
Asset location	V	0 to 75 bps
Spending strategy (withdrawal order)	VI	0 to 110 bps
Total-return versus income investing	VII	> 0 bps*
Total potential value added		*About 3% in net returns*

* Value is deemed significant but too unique to each investor to quantify.
We believe implementing the Vanguard Advisor's Alpha framework can add about 3% in net returns for your clients and also allow you to differentiate your skills and practice. The actual amount of value added may vary significantly, depending on clients' circumstances.
Source: Vanguard.

Below are the different modules and the potential value-add, based on Vanguard's research, they can have on an individual's overall "costs". For reference, "bps" is defined as basis points – a "common unit of measure for interest rates and other percentages in finance. One basis point is equal to 1/100th of 1%, or 0.01%, or 0.0001, and is used to denote the percentage change in a financial instrument."

Module I. Asset Allocation
- **Definition** "The percentage of a portfolio invested in various asset classes such as stocks, bonds, and cash

investments, according to the investor's financial situation, risk tolerance, and time horizon."
- **Potential Value-Add** "Value is deemed significant but too unique to each investor to quantify, based on each investor's varying time horizon, risk tolerance, and financial goals."

Module II. Cost-Effective Implementation
- **Definition** Ensuring an advisor is conscious of costs (expense ratios, trading or frictional costs, and taxes) when implementing an investment management strategy.
- **Potential Value-Add** "40 bps annually, by moving to low-cost funds. This value-add is the difference between the average investor experience, measured by the asset-weighted expense ratio of the entire mutual fund and ETF industry, and the lowest-cost funds within the universe. This value could be larger if using higher-cost funds than the asset-weighted averages"

Module III. Rebalancing
- **Definition** "The process of realigning the weightings of a portfolio of assets. Periodically buying or selling assets in a portfolio to maintain an original or desired level of asset allocation or risk."
- **Potential Value-Add** "Up to 35 bps when risk-adjusting a 60% stock/40% bond portfolio that is rebalanced annually versus the same portfolio that is not rebalanced"

Module IV. Behavioral Coaching
- **Definition** Helping clients maintain a long-term perspective and a disciplined approach to their financial plan.

- **Potential Value-Add** "Based on a Vanguard study of actual client behavior, we found that investors who deviated from their initial retirement fund investment trailed the target-date fund benchmark by 150 bps. This suggests that the discipline and guidance that an advisor might provide through behavioral coaching could be the largest potential value-add of the tools available to advisors. In addition, Vanguard research and other academic studies have concluded that behavioral coaching can add 1% to 2% in net return."

Module V. Asset Location
- **Definition** "The allocation of assets between taxable and tax-advantaged accounts" (e.g. individual accounts, Roth IRA accounts, 401(k) accounts, IRA accounts, Joint accounts, etc.).
- **Potential Value-Add** "0 to 75 bps, depending on the investor's asset allocation and "bucket" size (the breakdown of assets between taxable and tax-advantaged accounts). The majority of the benefits occur when the taxable and tax-advantaged accounts are roughly equal in size, the target allocation is in a balanced portfolio, and the investor is in a high marginal tax bracket. If an investor has all of his or her assets in one account type (that is, all taxable or all tax-advantaged), the value of asset location is 0 bps."

Module VI. Withdrawal Order for Client Spending from Portfolios
- **Definition** The order in which clients withdraw money from their different account types.
- **Potential Value-Add** "Up to 110 bps, depending on the investor's "bucket" size (the breakdown of assets between taxable and tax-advantaged accounts) and

marginal tax bracket. The greatest benefits occur when the taxable and tax-advantaged accounts are roughly equal in size and the investor is in a high marginal tax bracket. If an investor has all of his or her assets in one account type (that is, all taxable or all tax-advantaged), or an investor is not currently spending from the portfolio, the value of the withdrawal order is 0 bps."

Module VII. Total-Return Versus Income Investing
- **Definition** Total return is the rate of return an investment has over a given period of time. This includes capital gains, dividends, interest, and distributions. Income Investing is a strategy that involves assembling a portfolio of income-producing assets that generate dependable cash payouts.
- **Potential Value-Add** "Value is deemed significant but too unique to each investor to quantify, based on each investor's desired level of spending and the composition of his or her current portfolio."

Please note, while Vanguard shows a potential value-add of roughly 3% in net returns, the value an advisor can bring to a client is going to be unique to each case. A strategy that works for one individual may not be the best option for the next client. This is why following practice standards is extremely important as it provides the necessary information to create the most appropriate recommendations for each client and their unique situation.

While the whitepaper is specific to Vanguard's research, the broad strategies they discuss are not proprietary or unique. The strategies discussed above are available for any advisor to use when working with clients. When advisors utilize a holistic approach and take the time to discuss the different strategies available to clients, it will help differentiate them from other advisors while conveying the value they can add to the advisor-client relationship.

At the beginning of this chapter, we discussed the practice standards and best practices that advisors should be applying when engaging with clients, with one of those being *Understanding an Individual's Personal and Financial Situation*. Specifically, with respect to an individual's projected lifespan and healthspan.

The problem is, expected duration of life in the world of financial planning has thus far been based on averages – even for fiduciaries that are supposed to place the interests of their clients above everything else. There has been no effort whatsoever in the financial services industry to estimate healthspan – even though this should be a critical element to post-retirement planning. Advisors tend to err on the conservative side and recommend a client plan for a longer-than-average retirement. This makes sense at one level as the advisor doesn't want to be on the hook on the off chance a client lives to age 95 or 100 and is on the verge of depleting their assets, but this assumption often places an undue burden on the client.

Using an ultra-conservative averaging assumption for life expectancy isn't necessarily a bad approach; it's just that *most of the time it will be wrong*. For example, in a scenario where a plan was created assuming the client lives to 95, but they pass away at age 90, we can expect that they would be left with a *Positive Wealthspan*. But lifespan is much more than an estimation of how long someone is likely to live, and it needs to be considered in probabilistic terms relative to a spouse and the expected duration of healthspan. Lifespan needs to be a consideration when planning for strategies and recommendations, including but not limited to healthcare expenses, when to collect Social Security, estate planning, taxes, and planning for surviving spouses.

It's important to understand that it's easy to use this strategy for longer-than-average retirements, but we also need to consider scenarios when someone is not expected to live to 95 or 100; which will be most of the time depending on the current age of a client. Providing clients with realistic science-based estimates and options will allow both the client and advisor to plan for different scenarios; and together they can choose a plan that generates the most comfort for the client.

While women tend to live longer than men, this is not always the case, and always assuming this is a mistake waiting to happen. A widow or widower will have a lot to consider when their partner passes, so having a plan in place well in advance that both partners agree upon will significantly help reduce the stress that comes with such an event.

A financial plan should also consider life cycle changes such as life insurance needs, a loss in income, and a change in social security to name a few. It's also important to work with your financial planner, CPA, and estate attorney to ensure your estate is tax-efficient should a death occur. There is preferential treatment spouses receive from an estate perspective, making it vital that clients understand what to do once the situation arises. Having a plan in place ensures the clients are taking advantage of the benefits available to them.

Social Security is also directly connected to a reliable estimate of lifespan. Social Security is a form of "public" insurance funded by payroll taxes on wages earned and self-employment income. Traditionally, individuals who have earned the required number of credits are eligible for Social Security benefits. Based on the year a taxpayer was born, the

SSA designates a "full retirement age" for each person – this is when a person is entitled to full or unreduced retirement benefits. Individuals have the option to begin drawing on their benefit as early as age 62 and as late as age 70.

If a taxpayer starts collecting their benefit prior to their full retirement age, it will be at a reduced amount depending on how early they take it. If they delay collecting Social Security, they are eligible to increase their benefit by 8% for each year the delay occurs, until age 70. Assuming taxpayers collect Social Security until the end of life, it's apparent that expected lifespan is a critical factor used to decide when to begin collecting Social Security benefits.

It's important to note, lifespan isn't the only factor to consider when drawing Social Security. Other factors are important such as anticipated additional income after retirement.

As indicated earlier, most advisors use a conservative approach when estimating lifespan for the sake of running a financial plan. Since it is common to choose an expected lifespan of between 90-100 for everyone; the advice given most often is to delay turning on Social Security until age 70 when the benefit is the highest it can be. For many people, this is bad advice, and it is especially harmful guidance when both members of a couple are eligible for Social Security, and large differences in survival are expected between them.

For example, assume that the Wealthspan calculator estimates lifespan for a husband at 80 years and his wife at 95 years. In this case, it might not make sense for the husband to delay taking Social Security until age 68, while his spouse would be encouraged to delay taking Social Security until age 70. If averaging assumptions are used instead of a science-based approach, the couple would likely be missing out on the use of a source of income during a time in life when they can enjoy it the most – together.

One final topic that should not be missed is the idea of a living financial plan. Planning, as outlined here, is a complicated process of putting together the best recommendations based on what we know today and what we anticipate might happen in the future. However, life and financial markets have a way of throwing curve balls at the best laid plans, so an advisor and his/her client must consider the plan to be alive and flexible so unknown and unexpected events can be accounted for.

By way of example, maybe the plan was to pull required income from your investment accounts for the first three years of your retirement. However, if the markets are in the middle of large losses and your accounts are realizing paper losses as well, it may be prudent to change the plan during the market down-turn to draw income from a different source, like an annuity or the cash value of life insurance, so you aren't further drawing down accounts that are being negatively impacted by adverse market conditions. This small shift would allow your investment accounts to remain untouched and recover from the market losses before you begin to tap into those accounts again to meet your income needs.

Our goal throughout this chapter was to shed light on the importance of having a financial plan in place and to ensure individuals are working with financial professionals who understand the importance of taking a holistic approach to financial planning. We all know life has a weird way of keeping us on our toes and we hope there's now a better understanding of the importance of how and why we need to plan for the known and unknown events that may come our way.

Chapter 11. Tax Planning

Kirk Ashburn

A longer lifespan is something that some people should begin planning for, but while appealing if those added years are healthy, this scenario does add unique challenges for retirement planning. This can be especially true when considering tax planning and the need to produce greater after-tax wealth to achieve investment objectives required for *Positive Wealthspan*.

Personal attributes of individuals and couples, such as the presence or absence of genetic longevity traits, differences in anticipated longevity age by gender, and the presence or absence of healthy lifestyle choices, have significant effects (positive and negative) on our lifespan and healthspan. These factors also have an equally important impact on tax planning, with multiple strategies available that can be tailored to the personal needs of the client.

Taxes are one of the largest expenses that investors will face in their retirement years. They have lasting effects on surviving spouses if not anticipated in advance – a fact that is often overlooked by investors. A 2019 survey by the Nationwide Retirement Institute found that 39% of retirees that had been retired for 10+ years, did not consider how taxes would affect their retirement income at the time they were planning for retirement.

In this same study, 38% of future retirees surveyed agreed with the statement "I am terrified of what taxes will do to my retirement income." Despite those fears, 2 of every 5 people surveyed rarely consider the taxes they are paying or will pay in retirement and only 1 in 8 strongly agreed that they know how to use tax planning to get a desired outcome during tax season.[2]

One important reason why tax planning falls through the cracks is that it's difficult to do. There is always some level of uncertainty about the future, whether at a political or legislative level, regarding things like public policy, tax reform, and future tax rates, or even at a personal level such as a material unexpected expense or life event, additional income streams, excess capital gains, etc.

Regardless, there are some reasonable assumptions that can be made about the future of taxes. For example, it's reasonable to assume that taxes will rise in the future. It is safe to assume that as national debt continues to skyrocket amid

---

[2] https://mutualfunds.nationwide.com/nationwide-retirement-institute/tax-efficient-planning/survey-results

the government's response to the Coronavirus pandemic, the United States will continue to face rising federal budget deficits and underfunded government entitlement programs – at the same time tax rates remain near historic lows.

Even if tax rates were to remain stable in the future, individuals cannot predict what their personal tax rate will be in retirement given that it's likely to vary from one year to the next. Many investors currently assume that their tax rate will fall when they are no longer working, but in most cases, retirees are likely to face similar or higher taxes after they retire; making tax planning today an essential part of the equation for achieving *Positive Wealthspan*.

In this chapter, I will cover a few of the key concepts that investors should understand when navigating the complex world of tax planning. We'll also explore some common strategies to reduce lifetime tax liability, with the goal of achieving a tax-free retirement and a multigenerational *Positive Wealthspan*.

Creating Tax Diversification

In our working years, often the only major tax strategy considered is maximizing contributions to your retirement plan, thereby decreasing your taxable income. Maybe you were a more prudent saver and had also socked away additional assets by opening and contributing to a Roth IRA or brokerage account. In assessing your current tax situation, having a firm grasp on your current account or asset mix under different account types; and planning for additional contributions; can be crucial as each will be treated differently both pre-and post-retirement.

- **Tax-Deferred Accounts (Traditional IRA, 401(k) plans, 403(b) plans, 457 plans, Simple IRA and others):** In the case of tax-deferred assets, these account types allow you to realize immediate tax deductions up to the full amount of your contribution and allow assets to grow tax deferred. Down the road after you reach retirement age, taxes are assessed at your ordinary income rate when funds are withdrawn.
- In most cases, normal distributions will incur a penalty for early withdrawals before age 59½, and mandatory taxable distributions will occur after reaching age 70½ (Note: The SECURE Act of 2019 changed the Required Distribution Age from 70½ to 72 for those that reach 70½ in 2020 or beyond). These Required Minimum Distribution (RMD) amounts are determined by dividing your tax-deferred account balances as of December 31 of the previous

year by a life expectancy factor determined by the IRS. These assets are taxed as ordinary income.
- These distributions may increase year over year and can pose some risks from a tax perspective. If not planned for carefully, the additional income may move an investor into a higher tax bracket in a given year. Any undistributed assets would be fully exposed to any future rate hikes or a change to filing status (Married filing jointly to single for example). Additionally, your spousal beneficiaries will be required to take forced taxable distributions over their lifetime, which can lead to a significant increase in their tax burden if not planned for.
- **Tax-Exempt Accounts (Roth IRA, Roth 401(k) and others):** These accounts are funded on an after-tax basis and grow tax-free. Unlike tax-deferred assets, as taxes have already been paid, when you start making withdrawals in retirement you owe nothing — not even for the earnings on your investments. The money is yours, free and clear (with no mandatory withdrawals to boot).
- You may withdraw your contributions to a Roth IRA penalty-free at any time for any reason, but you'll be

penalized for withdrawing any investment earnings before age 59½, unless it's for a qualifying reason.

- From an estate planning perspective, there are also some advantages as these assets will transfer to a surviving spouse or beneficiary without income tax costs and will allow them to continue to withdraw or grow the assets tax-free over their lifetime if desired. A non-spouse beneficiary will be required to take mandatory tax-free minimum distributions over their lifetime, thus preventing disruption of their personal income tax management.

- **Taxable Accounts (Individual/Brokerage, Savings, and others):** For taxable accounts, investors must pay tax on any income received - dividends, interest, and rent on real estate – as well as any gains realized on the sale of a security in the year it was received. The return of principal is not taxable, and withdrawals can occur at any point in time. Depending on the type of dividend paid (qualified vs non-qualified), issuer of the bond initiating the interest payment (corporate or treasury bonds vs states or municipalities), or the duration of time the securities were held prior to sale (less than one year vs longer than one year), the prevailing tax rates may vary. For example, dividends paid by companies from after-tax profits (i.e. qualified dividends) or gains on the sale of securities held for a period of longer than one year would be taxed at a lower, more preferential tax rate with a maximum rate of 20% as opposed to ordinary income tax rates, which could be substantially higher.

- One important tax advantage to keep in mind occurs when securities in taxable accounts are passed on to a beneficiary at death. When the assets are transferred, the cost basis (the original purchase price) of property transferred at death receives a "step-up" in basis to its fair market value. This eliminates an heir's capital gains tax liability on appreciation in the property's value that occurred during the decedent's lifetime. For example, an investor purchasing shares at $5 and leaving them to an heir when the shares are currently valued at $20 raises the cost basis for the shares to the current market price of $20. Any capital gains tax paid in the future will be based on the $20 cost basis, not on the original purchase price of $5.

While the ideal tax optimization strategy would involve maximizing contributions to both tax-deferred and tax-exempt accounts, there are certain variables to consider if such allocations are not possible. As a general rule of thumb, in the pre-retirement stage, low-income earners or those who expect to be in a higher tax bracket during retirement than they are currently, are encouraged to focus on funding a tax-exempt account. At this stage, contributions to a tax-deferred account may not prove to be as advantageous as the current tax benefit would be minimal in the case of low-income earners, while future obligation may be significantly larger. Increasing Roth IRA contributions can also offer some spending flexibility in retirement, since you can withdraw money without increasing your tax bill and you won't have to take annual RMDs, unlike a Traditional IRA or other tax-deferred vehicles.

On the flipside, higher-salary earners or those who believe their tax bracket may be lower in retirement should focus on contributions to a tax-deferred account such as a 401(k) or traditional IRA. The immediate benefit can lower their marginal tax bracket while potentially reducing their overall tax liability as future withdrawals would be taxed at a lower tax rate.

Being mindful of the tax status of assets in retirement, and how funds are allocated among them, is an important aspect of planning when considering potential tax exposure in the future. Just as investment diversification is often preached, tax diversification deserves commensurate attention. This allows flexibility to draw income from different sources depending on your tax situation and changes in overall life circumstances. When considering the two alternatives, just remember that you are always going to pay taxes, and depending on the type of account, it's simply a question of when. However, if future tax rates are expected to be higher and people find themselves in higher tax brackets in the future, and we would advise our clients to operate under both assumptions; there is something to be said for tax-free retirement savings.

RMD Planning and Roth Conversions

One common trap many investors often find themselves in is sitting on a large bucket of tax-deferred assets. The good news for those folks is that they've done a great job in saving and growing a nest egg! The bad news is this can also come at a significant cost to them and their heirs down the road.

When you withdraw money from tax-deferred accounts, it will be taxed as ordinary income in the calendar year in which you make the withdrawal. If unexpected withdrawals are necessary – i.e. you need extra funds for a vacation, purchasing a new car, or helping a family member, the excess funds withdrawn may bump you into a higher tax bracket.

In addition to withdrawals from tax-deferred accounts being taxed as ordinary income, they can also affect how much of your Social Security income is taxed. Each withdrawal may make more of your Social Security income subject to taxation as additional IRA withdrawals increase the amount of 'other income' that is considered when calculating taxes on your benefit – a surprise to most. A few retirees find they pay over 40 cents in taxes per dollar of IRA withdrawals because their IRA withdrawals cause more of their Social Security to be taxed.

Lastly, the required minimum distributions associated with these accounts can create a tax nightmare, as these withdrawals are taxed as ordinary income. This means that withdrawals will count toward your total taxable income for the year and may push you into a higher tax bracket or impact the taxes you pay on your Social Security or Medicare.

There are a few ways to reduce the tax exposure that comes with RMDs, such as continuing to work past the age of 72 or donating distributions to a qualified charity. But perhaps the most popular strategy to avoid drawing down required distributions would be converting these assets to a

Roth IRA. This can not only help in reducing future RMDs and their associated tax consequences, but also solve some of the additional complications identified earlier in this section related to taxation of social security and future unexpected withdrawals. As discussed previously, unlike traditional IRAs whose distributions are taxed, their Roth counterparts generally come with tax-free distributions once you reach age 59½ and come with no required minimum distributions. Additionally, when your beneficiaries inherit a traditional IRA, they'll owe income taxes on the amounts withdrawn – remember, the government still wants its cut. But if they inherit a Roth IRA, they won't. You've already paid the tax for them when you contributed to the account or converted your traditional IRA.

The largest disadvantage of converting is that contributions aren't tax-deductible the way they are with traditional IRAs or 401(k) plans. That means if you move pre-tax money from one of those accounts to a Roth IRA, you must pay taxes on the amount. If, for example, you have $200,000 in a traditional IRA and convert that amount to a Roth IRA, you would owe $48,000 in taxes (assuming you're in the 24% tax bracket), a hefty amount. Convert enough and it could even push you into a higher tax bracket.

To minimize this burden, rather than taking the tax hit all at once, Wealthspan Advisors may establish a multi-year conversion strategy to spread out the tax cost over many years and avoid the potential of bumping you up to a higher tax bracket. This situation cannot always be avoided completely but considering these strategies early on can pay huge dividends in the future.

Although there are some additional factors to ponder, the current low tax cost for converting, with tax rates at all-time lows, plus the creation of 'insurance' against higher tax rates in future years on income that will accumulate, creates the perfect storm for the Roth conversion strategy leading the way to a tax-free retirement.

Life Insurance as an Added Layer of Tax Diversification

In addition to the typical retirement accounts outlined above, something that is typically not seen as synonymous with retirement or tax planning is life insurance, specifically permanent life insurance. This can play a significant role for you and your beneficiaries and can offer as much, or as little, tax-free income in retirement as you are willing to plan and save for.

Permanent life insurance policies not only provide death benefit coverage, but also include a cash-value component that can allow the policyholder to build up a substantial amount of tax-deferred savings over time. With permanent life insurance policies, the gain in the cash value is generally tax-deferred, allowing your assets to grow over time as you pay premiums. The policyholder can also access the cash value of the policy on a tax-advantaged basis. Money taken from the cash value of a life insurance policy is not subject to taxes up to the "cost basis" – the amount paid into the policy through premiums. In addition, the policy holder has the option to borrow against his cash value at any time. The amount borrowed will not be taxable as income, even if it is in excess of his cost basis.

As is the case with most forms of life insurance, upon the death of the insured, the death benefit is generally paid out income tax free to a properly named beneficiary (or beneficiaries).

A few additional benefits of life insurance include the fact that for those who may be retiring early (prior to age 59½), there are no early withdrawal penalties for removing funds, unlike with IRAs and other retirement accounts. Likewise, there are no required minimum distribution rules for leaving funds in such policies past age 70½, as there are with many qualified retirement plans and traditional IRAs.

Because of the numerous tax advantages available on cash-value life insurance policies, some individuals can use them as tools in areas of financial planning. For example, many retirees are using their life insurance cash values to fill the income gap that may be left when the funds from their retirement accounts and Social Security do not cover all of their expenses. In this case, funds from a policy loan can be especially beneficial as they not only help bridge that gap but are received income tax-free and don't have a negative impact on the taxation of Social Security income.

Optimizing Your Asset Location

With these varying account types and vehicles in mind, many investors (and advisors) fail to consider the location within which investment assets or investment methodologies are used when constructing a portfolio. This is something that can have a significant impact on lifetime tax liability. A typical investor with a balanced portfolio consisting of 60% stocks and 40% bonds might hold investments in both taxable accounts and tax-deferred accounts. Although the investor's overall portfolio should be balanced, each account does not need to have the same asset mix or strategy. Doing so ignores the tax advantages of each type of account that will assure the best after-tax return. This is where having a smart asset allocation strategy can prove beneficial.

So, which investments do you put where to increase tax efficiency within your portfolio? Asset location benefits will vary based on a multitude of factors, and will differ for each investor, and must be balanced between the anticipated tax efficiency of the investment and the expected returns. Although each situation can be different, Figure 7 below provides a general framework for different investment types and an appropriate location from a tax perspective.

	Tax treatment of expected returns	Taxable	Tax-deferred	Tax-exempt
Tax-free municipal securities and municipal mutual funds	Exempt	✓	✓	✓
Equity securities held long-term for growth	Taxed at long-term capital gain rates	✓	✓	✓
Equity index funds/ETFs (other than REITs)		✓	✓	✓
Tax-managed mutual funds and managed accounts		✓	✓	✓
Real estate investment trusts (REITs)	Generally, 80% of income taxed at ordinary rates; 20% tax-exempt	✓	✓	✓
High-turnover stock mutual funds that deliver effectively all returns as short-term capital gains	Taxed at ordinary income rates	✓	✓	✓
Fully taxable bonds and bond funds (i.e., corporates)		✓	✓	✓

✓ More appropriate   ✓ Appropriate   ✓ Less appropriate

Source: https://www.fidelity.com/viewpoints/investing-ideas/asset-location-lower-taxes

For example, if you own fixed-income investments such as bonds or are implementing a managed income model, it may make more sense to hold them in tax-deferred accounts. Interest payments on these positions are often taxed as ordinary income and therefore wouldn't be the best option when used in a taxable account. Additionally, capital appreciation on these funds is typically muted in comparison to equity related holdings designed to limit future tax liabilities. On the flipside, high-turnover equity related funds or portfolios may be a better fit in tax-exempt vehicles, such as a Roth IRA with no capital gain or RMD headaches down the road.

For long-term, passively managed strategies or tax efficient positions like stocks and ETFs, taxable accounts are preferred. The capital gains from these types of investments are taxed only when you make a withdrawal, which could be decades in the future and are generally taxed at a lower rate. Things like municipal bonds may also find a home in taxable accounts due to the tax-free nature of the income received. However, due to the low yield and rising interest rate environment we find ourselves in, this may not be the most attractive option.

Asset location is relatively straightforward in principle. However, the implementation and ongoing portfolio management, particularly in retirement, can quickly make things complex.

Tax Withdrawal Strategies

As you approach and enter retirement, your financial situation changes, presenting some unique challenges and opportunities. When steady income from employment stops, it's replaced with other sources, such as social security, pensions, and investments. This opens up a lot of doors, but also comes with additional complications. You can usually control when to start these income sources and, in the case of investments, decide from which account to pull money, as different accounts may have different tax consequences.

When it comes to planning for retirement income, in addition to any social security income streams, the conventional wisdom is that retirees should take money from accounts in the following order:

1. Taxable
2. Tax deferred
3. Tax free

The motivation behind this conventional wisdom is to preserve tax-deferred assets for as long as possible. However, depending on an individual's tax situation, the conventional wisdom may not always be the best course of action. For example, if you have substantial unrealized capital gains on taxable assets, it may be better to withdraw funds from tax-deferred or tax-free (e.g., Roth IRA) accounts first. By doing so, you may be able to preserve all or a significant amount of your taxable assets, which could then be passed to your heirs with a "stepped-up" cost basis.

Alternatively, it may make sense to time the withdrawal of funds from tax-deferred accounts for years when you're likely to be in a lower tax bracket compared with your pre-retirement tax bracket. These years could occur early in retirement before required minimum distributions (RMDs) from retirement accounts begin, or later in retirement when medical expenses may be higher. Drawing from tax-deferred accounts when your tax rate is low will allow you to enjoy the full benefit of the lower rate.

An additional example of a smart withdrawal strategy may be to pull income from different tax sources as you gradually transition from lower to higher tax brackets. That is, draw enough income from tax-deferred sources such as traditional IRAs or 401(k)s to reach the limit of the income tax bracket, maximizing the use of the lower tax bracket for ordinary income. This also reduces the balance of tax-deferred accounts, which lowers required minimum distributions in the future. As more income is needed, consider drawing from other sources (taxable or tax-free) to avoid increasing ordinary income, which is subject to higher tax rates.

Optimizing withdrawals in retirement is a complex process that requires a thorough understanding of tax situations, financial goals, how accounts are structured, and the unique life and health circumstances projected for each client. It's important to take the time to make a plan to manage withdrawals and re-evaluate your plan regularly, as it may vary from one year to the next.

Tax Loss Harvesting

One final concept to consider when trying to manage your tax bill is something called tax loss harvesting. Everyone has winners and losers in the positions they hold in their taxable accounts. However, if you have some long-term winners that have amassed a large capital gain and would be taxable if a withdrawal was made, it often makes sense to liquidate the losers in your portfolio to offset some of the gains on the winners.

This can be done at any time of the year, but most people look at this near the end of a calendar year to get it done so the transactions can be claimed on the tax return for that year. This strategy allows you to create a tax-free income source.

Consider the following example. Let's say you owned Apple stock for many years and have a good amount of gains on the stock that would be treated as long-term capital gains and generally taxed at 15%, depending on your tax bracket. We'll also assume you have held General Electric Company stock for the past several years and have seen significant losses on that stock position. In this case, you have the opportunity to sell $25,000 worth of Apple stock at a significant gain and sell $25,000 worth of General Electric stock at a significant loss and have those gains and losses offset, creating a tax-free distribution of $50,000 from your account.

Tax Considerations for Surviving Spouses

As discussed in Chapter 4, we know that women typically outlive men. The tax planning that most advisors are concerned with only relates to planning for income for the couple. But what happens when a spouse dies? How is income and taxation impacted when that happens?

We may find through our couples' analysis of health and survival that the wife could outlive her husband by 20 years or more. Under these conditions, it is critically important to consider the tax changes that are likely to occur at the death of a spouse.

While both spouses are alive, they likely each receive Social Security income. However, when a spouse dies, the surviving spouse loses the lesser of the two Social Security payments. The surviving spouse also loses the ability to file a joint tax return, so the exemption amount is cut in half. What the spouse may gain is a large IRA on which RMD's are due, in addition to the RMD that is likely being taken on their own IRA. The income from these RMD payments along with the lower exemption amount may move the surviving spouse into a higher tax bracket and cause more of the Social Security income to be taxed, further increasing the negative tax situation.

Many of the strategies discussed in this chapter, like Roth IRA conversion and the use of life insurance to create a tax-free income stream, may be most beneficial for a surviving spouse. Peace of mind is achieved for a surviving spouse when they know where the income that they need to live will come from, and that it is properly structured to avoid a tax burden that brings confusion and stress following the difficult time after the loss.

Smarter tax planning can truly be life changing for many people financially throughout the course of their retirement.

No different than planning for, or assessing our personal well-being or longevity, there are many things to consider when it comes to taxes that influence your ability to achieve *Positive Wealthspan*.

Each person's personal situation is unique and can change over time. Your tax plan is no different. Customizing a tax plan for you and assessing that plan regularly can give you flexibility and a surprising level of control over future tax bills, putting you on a great path to financial success.

Chapter 12. Better Planning Works

Theodore M. Homa

Ten years ago, I faced one of the most difficult challenges imaginable. At the age of 62, I was told that my heart was failing and that without a transplant, I would not survive long. My condition was immediately serious enough to require the implantation of an artificial heart. Surviving the surgery itself was just the first of many challenges. Many patients my age fail to even wake up from the procedure. If lucky enough to survive having my own diseased heart permanently removed from my body and replaced by a machine, I would then be placed on the heart transplant list where my only hope was that a match could be found in enough time to save my life.

Six months later, a match became available. So now a new set of hurdles stood before me. Surviving through another traumatic surgical challenge and the one I faced months earlier, as it turns out, was only half the battle. The problem in my case; or at least the unusual circumstance I faced, was that I knew too much about my own condition.

Until this news arrived, I was a practicing geriatrician with a thriving practice, so I knew all too well the challenges I was about to face because I had been advising my own patients for decades on their personal health challenges – some easier to handle than my condition, but some worse as well. However, instead of giving advice and counsel, I was on the receiving end. I experienced first-hand what happens when a part of the body fails. With only one heart and no redundancy as is the case with other organs such as kidneys and lungs, I knew all too well what the consequences of failure would be.

Because of my training, I had a good idea of what to expect during the surgeries, but I had no idea what to expect if I survived having a heart removed from my body, twice. My chances of surviving both surgeries were not good. If that happened, would I be debilitated in any way? How would my cognitive functioning be influenced? Would I have enough money to live life as my wife and I did before this challenge presented itself; and if so, how long would that money last?

Most important to me personally, would I be able to practice medicine again? Even if I survived the transplant, the medications used to avoid rejection placed me in a difficult position since my own patients posed a threat to my health. These questions weighed heavily on me in the months between my diagnosis and the moment I awakened from the gift of a new heart.

I was going to embark on this journey of survival no matter what, but I needed to know in advance how I was going to deal with some of these challenges should I be fortunate enough to survive. A trip to my financial advisor's office revealed something I did not anticipate; or at least I didn't remember. When I met with my advisor 20 years ago, we established a plan for the future that was designed to maintain my anticipated income stream should I become debilitated.

Losing any of my mental or physical capacity to operate as a practicing geriatrician meant that my income would likely decline to zero with little or no chance of recovery. In my profession it's often an all or none proposition. My advisor and apparently, I as well, knew this back then, so together we hatched a plan that would protect me, and my family should I face a debilitating or catastrophic illness or even death. I did not remember doing this.

The bottom line was that my advisor set up a series of disability income insurance policies for me that would ensure my income stream for an extended period, should I face any catastrophic illness. When the math behind our decision-making some 20 years earlier was revealed to my wife and I by our advisor, one huge burden was immediately lifted off of our family's shoulders. If I died during this ordeal, my family would have been well cared for; but critically important to me was what would happen if I survived? Could we continue to live life as we had in the past? Would I be able to use those funds to facilitate my entrance back into the field of medicine? The answer was a resounding YES! With this financial burden taken care of through sound financial planning, I could then concentrate on coming back to my new normal rather than wondering how we would survive in a world that could be far different from the one I was used to.

I'm here writing this chapter now with a mental acuity that is as good as or better than where I was before my diagnosis. I'm practicing geriatric medicine again; having recovered fully from both traumatic surgeries and the long recovery process associated with them. My family's income stream was uninfluenced by these traumatic events; allowing us to live our lives to the fullest without any financial concerns at all. The peace of mind that followed my post diagnosis meeting with my financial advisor cannot be emphasized enough as a critical element in my recovery and rebound.

There is no doubt in my mind that I'm here today, thriving with the gift of a new heart, because I had the financial resources that afforded me access to the best medical care, and which allowed me to take the time to recover all of my mental and physical faculties – with zero interruption in my family's quality of life. My life has returned to as normal as is possible post-transplant surgery, in large measure, due to a set of financial planning decisions made years earlier.

My story is unique at one level because organ transplants are relatively rare by comparison to all of the other health challenges faced by our rapidly aging world. What isn't unique, or particularly surprising, is the value of financial planning early in life. While it's never too late to begin this planning process, it is also never too early. The planning process that I went through 20 years ago, is exactly the same process that everyone should be going through today. Whether you're just starting out your career, at the apex of your accomplishments, approaching retirement, or already in retirement, assessing your future and planning for various contingencies can be life changing.

My financial planner had the good sense to develop a plan for me that was ideally suited to my career trajectory, but there was no way for anyone to know at the time that I would face a catastrophic illness two decades later. While it is not possible to forecast the future with precision, it is possible to use science as the basis for a more informed decision in today's world. In this regard, my experience of peace of mind after having learned about our wise planning decades earlier, can be achieved by anyone at any age, today, using common sense and advanced planning.

The irony is that the suggestion that planning ahead works to extend and enhance life, is the same advice I give my patients. For example, there is ample evidence to demonstrate that the use of tobacco is harmful to health – reducing lifespan by 10 years. Cigarette and cigar smoking are linked to lung cancer, head and neck cancers, even bladder cancer. The choice to be healthy at any age requires the avoidance of these and other harmful behavioral risk factors.

Financial planning is not my field, so I dare not give advice in this area. But as it turns out, the extension of healthy life that I help create for my patients, requires the formulation of a personal plan that resembles the one created for your financial future by your advisor. The benefits of planning turned out ideal for me – even when faced with severe health challenges. However, the message is the same whether it's personal health or personal finances – start early, and it's never too late.

Chapter 13. Life as a Wealthspan Client and Advisor

Kirk Ashburn

Throughout this book we have attempted to make a clear point that achieving a *Positive Wealthspan* is critically important and, with the use of science-based personal assessments and proper planning, it can be achieved. There are, of course, some changes that are likely in order to put you in a position to achieve the goal of *Positive Wealthspan*.

Many advisors sell products, most do not implement plans. Many advisors use a generic life expectancy if they are doing any type of planning with clients, with little regard for what is unique about you that separates you from average. Most advisors don't discuss or plan for the differences in lifespan for spouses and the many changes that a surviving spouse faces if not prepared.

But it doesn't have to be that way!

Working with an advisor equipped with new, breakthrough science and technology and trained on how to use the information gained through these tools can make all the difference in whether or not you achieve a *Positive Wealthspan*.

Gaining an understanding of your unique lifespan and healthspan is the first step in the process. From that starting point, you should work with a fiduciary advisor well versed in a planning process that addresses:

- the timing of taking Social Security;
- how much risk you should take;
- which financial products should be used;
- which account type should hold each financial product for maximum tax efficiency;
- where you should pull income from for the best tax management;
- what you should do to create a legacy plan so that assets can be passed on exactly as you wish.

The advisors associated with Wealthspan Advisors utilize a unique planning process that you likely haven't ever seen before from any other advisor. Because we're intimately aware of the foundational piece of longevity estimate and how it drives many decisions when building a financial plan, we created a process that we call A.T.O.M.I.C. planning, inspired by our scientific approach to wealth management.

A – Assess. We review the current assets, income sources, expenses, goals and hopes for clients to get a good understanding of the financial path they are on currently.

T – Teach. We teach clients about the positives and negatives of their current financial products and situation. We provide a complete understanding of the risk and return dynamics of their current holdings and talk about what should be expected if clients remain on the path they're currently on. This includes a probability of success analysis, which tells a client how likely they are to achieve their financial goals if they continue on the same path.

We find clients, like you, have a better chance at making good financial decisions if they have a good understanding of their current situation, so they have something to compare other options to.

O – Objectives. We talk with clients about what they would like to achieve. We discuss hopes and dreams to see if we can help make them become a reality. Sometimes we can't, but often we can create a plan that has better performance, lower fees and is more tax efficient so we can accomplish those objectives. However, we have to first identify where we want to go so we can develop a plan to get there.

M – Mitigation. Managing and mitigating risk is a big part of creating a plan that will be successful long-term. Sometimes that means we use smarter wealth management strategies to try to avoid large losses in the stock market. Sometimes that means using insurance or annuities to create a stream of income to last a lifetime or create a source of tax-free income so other assets don't need to be used for income creation. Sometimes it means building in an emergency fund to cover unexpected healthcare expenses or recommending a product called asset-based long-term care, which can be used if LTC is needed, but passed on to heirs if it isn't needed.

There are many ways to mitigate and manage risks, but the first step is to identify the risks that are likely to present themselves and then plan for them.

Jim Rohn is quoted as saying, *"The reason why most people face the future with apprehension instead of anticipation is because they don't have it well designed."* When risks are identified and mitigated, you can face the future with a good amount of peace and confidence.

I – Integrate. The process of integration is an implementation of a new plan. This likely doesn't mean we wipe the slate clean and start all over, but that we identify, as we work together, areas where improvements can be made, and we set out to put the new plan in motion. We say it that way because it will be a changing and evolving plan. Because markets and personal circumstances change, we need to be flexible, so we are always addressing challenges and taking advantage of opportunities.

C – Calibrate. This is a process of monitoring the plan and making small tweaks and changes as needed. For example, the plan may dictate that income be taken from an account that is invested in the stock market, but if the markets are experiencing a period of volatility or losses, it may make more sense to stop distributions from that account and begin distributions from a different, less volatile account. In doing so, we don't make losses worse by pulling money out of an account that is losing money.

It's a common-sense approach, but many advisors don't take the time to plan well, implement a good plan and then make smart adjustments along the way.

A *Positive Wealthspan* is within reach! As you have learned throughout this book, the foundation to a well-designed *Positive Wealthspan* is where aging science and wealth management intersect. The advisors of Wealthspan Advisors are aware of its importance, well trained in its application and work hard to help clients, like you, create, prepare for and live out the best retirement scenario possible. And, you shouldn't wait until you're in or near retirement to get started. Retirement planning is most successful when you start early.

We've already talked about the importance of health and happiness in retirement, and a well-designed plan can remove pressure that comes with unknown financial outcomes. We're all aware of how money worries can negatively impact health and happiness, so good planning and smart lifestyle decisions can help keep you healthy and happy.

Finally, the advisors of Wealthspan Advisors are honest and always put the interests of their clients first. We treat clients like family, where we only want the best for everyone we meet and have the privilege to serve.

It isn't our job or goal to sell anything to anyone. The implementation that leads to the purchase of financial products only happens when everyone understands how each product fits in the plan to accomplish the set objectives. All positives and negatives are on the table and discussed before any decisions are made.

Our goal is to make our clients feel comfortable throughout the planning process, where they play a big role in how the plan develops, so they can confidently retire and enjoy their *Positive Wealthspan*.

The journey to a *Positive Wealthspan* begins at mywealthspan.com. Please visit this site for more information.

IV. Concluding Remarks

There is an underlying theme behind this book, and it's probably not what you think. To emphasize the point here, I'm going to borrow language from a book I (Jay) published several years ago entitled *A Measured Breath of Life* (2013) – the title of the chapter is The Rhythms of Life and Death.

The sun rises and sets, seasons change, leaves fall to the ground, the Earth revolves around the Sun, the North Star always points north, and creatures like humans, dogs, mice, and elephants are born, grow up, grow old, and eventually die. The laws of nature that drive the biological functioning of our bodies operate with regularity, like clocks ticking in the background or the beat of our heart beneath our chest.

There is a comforting cadence to the rhythms of life – especially if we are attuned to their existence, and even if – quite frankly, it never seems to end well. But even with discrete bookends marking the beginning and ending of our lives, it's the quality and length of our journey through life that matters most, not the nature of our entrance and exit from it.

Paying attention to the cadence during the voyage

provides most of us with a sense of 'distance' from the start and 'proximity' to the end. Recognizing the cadence to life and death can enhance the journey by compelling us to stay in the moment. For some this can be a frightening realization.

Annie Besant (a British writer from the 19th century) once said: *"out of the darkness of the womb, into the darkness of the grave, man passes across his narrow strip of life. Two vast eternities stretch oceanlike on either side of the island of individual existence, and through the darkness that enshrouds them no human eye, it has been thought, could ever pierce."*

If life is thought of as a tiny island in the vast ocean of infinite time, then we each surface for a brief moment, take a measured breath of life's air, and then return forever to the calm.

This book is not really about wealth. It's not about retirement planning. It's not about reducing your tax burden. It's not about deciding about when to start Social Security. And it's not about life or health insurance. Well, at least these aren't the central theme.

Pursuing Wealthspan is about developing and maintaining a lifelong plan on how to acquire and keep the most precious commodities of all – health and happiness. There are many ways to do this of course, and we're not psychologists, so get off the couch.

The goal here is straightforward – put the tools of modern science to work to bring the world of financial planning into the 21st century; and by so doing, make it possible for financial advisors and their clients, for the first time, to utilize science-based assessment tools that will enable us all to determine just how far from average we are. The goal is to achieve what Hyman Roth could not – the maintenance of health through financial security that matches the duration of a long and healthy life.

When the plan behind a successful effort to achieve *Positive Wealthspan* comes together, there is a piece-of-mind that comes from having executed a well thought out life plan for the third phase of life. Life is too short to spend much of it worrying about anything other than enjoying each day and having the resources needed to allow you to pursue what makes you happy.

V. Acknowledgments

The editors would like to thank all of the authors for their thoughtful contributions to what we collectively see as a new movement in wealth management. Getting an entire industry to move into the 21st century in terms of how planning is done is difficult. This book is intended to illustrate how the merging of wealth management and aging science has the potential to revolutionize the industry – for the benefit of everyone. We're deeply appreciative of the effort put forth to bring this vision to reality.

> *This book is for informational purposes only and is not an offer or solicitation for the sale or purchase of any securities or advisory service. Exposure to ideas and the financial vehicles discussed are not investment advice or a recommendation to buy or sell any financial vehicle. This information is not tax or legal advice. Individuals should consult with the professionals specializing in the fields of tax, law, accounting, or investments regarding the applicability of this information to their situation. Past performance is not a guarantee of future results. Investments will fluctuate and when redeemed may be worth more or less than when originally invested.*

ABOUT THE AUTHORS

S. Jay Olshansky is co-founder and chief scientist at Lapetus Solutions, Inc., and Professor of Public Health at the University of Illinois at Chicago. Dr. Olshansky received his Ph.D. in Sociology/Demography at the University of Chicago in 1984; he's the first author of The Quest for Immortality: Science at the Frontiers of Aging (Norton, 2001); A Measured Breath of Life (2013); and The Rise of Generians (2020); and co-editor of Aging: The Longevity Dividend (Cold Spring Harbor Laboratory Press, 2015). He is on the Board of Directors of the American Federation for Aging Research and was on the Board of Scientific Advisors at PepsiCo. In 2016, Dr. Olshansky was honored with the Donald P. Kent Award from the Gerontological Society of America, the Irving S. Wright Award from the American Federation for Aging Research, and he was named a Next Avenue Influencer in Aging; in 2017 he received the Alvar Svanborg Award and in 2018 he received the Glenn Award from the Glenn Foundation for Medical Research.

Kirk Ashburn is a highly trained professional with more than 15 years of industry experience. He has successfully been involved in helping individuals and families in Illinois and across the country to change the way they save and plan for their future as well as generations to come. Kirk focuses on providing retirement income planning services with the goal of educating clients on their options for meeting their current financial needs, achieving their long-term financial goals, avoiding common retirement-planning mistakes and enjoying a lifetime of financial freedom. This approach helps his clients have confidence with their financial affairs, now and throughout their retirement.

Jeffrey Stukey is an Investment Adviser representative of Wealthspan Investment Management, LLC, a Michigan Registered Investment Adviser. Stukey has been in the financial services business for 20 years. Most of his time has been spent in executive level roles helping train hundreds of financial advisors around the country on how to better plan for and serve their clients. He has a deep understanding of financial planning and the financial products that can be used to create the desired outcome for clients. After watching his parents work hard but struggle financially for most of his childhood and early adult life, Jeff set out to help clients become more educated and get better advice to really help them grow and protect their wealth so they could live their best life. Because of the experience gained over the last 20 years, Jeff has been able to communicate well with clients, understand what they are trying to accomplish and help put them in a position to really thrive in and through retirement.

Dr. Austad is Distinguished Professor and Chair of the Department of Biology at the University of Alabama at Birmingham (UAB). He also directs UAB's Nathan Shock Center of Excellence in the Basic Biology of Aging and serves as Senior Scientific Director of the American Federation for Aging Research. After receiving his PhD from Purdue University, he held faculty appointments at Harvard University, the University of Idaho, and the University of Texas Health Science Center San Antonio before coming to UAB in 2014. Author of more than 200 scientific papers, 5 books, and more than 150 print and electronic media columns on science for the lay public, Dr. Austad's trade book, *Why We Age* (1999, John Wiley & Sons) has been translated into 8 languages. He serves on the External Advisory Board of the Mayo Clinic's Kogod Center on Aging, the University of Washington Nathan Shock Center, and the San Francisco-based Longevity Consortium. His research on aging has won multiple awards, including the Geron Corporation-Samuel Goldstein Distinguished Publication Award, the Nathan A. Shock Award from the National Institute on Aging, the Robert W. Kleemeier Award, the Purdue Outstanding Alumnus Award, the Fondation IPSEN Longevity Prize, and the Irving S. Wright Award of Distinction. He is an elected Fellow of the American

Association for the Advancement of Science and the Gerontological Society of America.

Dr. Ken Dychtwald, Founder & CEO of Age Wave. Over the past 40+ years, Ken Dychtwald has emerged as North America's foremost visionary and original thinker regarding the lifestyle, marketing, health care, and workforce implications of the age wave. Ken is a psychologist, gerontologist, and best-selling author of 17 books on aging and longevity-related issues, including *Bodymind*; *Age Wave: The Challenges and Opportunities of an Aging Society*; *A New Purpose: Redefining Money, Family, Work, Retirement, and Success* and his latest *What Retirees Want: A Holistic View of Life's Third Age*. Since 1986, Ken has been the Founder and CEO of Age Wave, a firm created to guide companies and government groups in product/service development for boomers and mature adults. His client list has included over half the Fortune 500. He has served as a fellow of the World Economic Forum and was a featured speaker at two White House Conferences on Aging. Ken has twice received the distinguished American Society on Aging Award for outstanding national leadership, and *American Demographics* honored him as the single most influential marketer to baby boomers over the past quarter century. His article in the *Harvard Business Review*, "It's Time to Retire Retirement," was awarded the prestigious McKinsey Award, tying for first place with the legendary Peter Drucker. He was honored by *Investment Advisor* as one of the 35 most influential thought leaders in the financial services industry over the past 35 years. Ken and his wife, Maddy, recently received the Esalen Prize for their outstanding contributions to advancing the human potential of aging men and women worldwide. In 2018 he was awarded the Inspire Award from the International Council on Active Aging for his exceptional and lasting contributions to the active-aging industry and for his efforts to make a difference in the lives of older adults globally. During his career, Ken has addressed more than two million people worldwide in his speeches to corporate, association, social service, and government groups. His strikingly accurate predictions and innovative ideas are regularly featured in leading print and electronic media worldwide and have garnered more than twelve billion media impressions. In addition to his role at Age Wave, he is deeply involved in numerous activities for the public good including serving as a member of the XPRIZE Board of Trustees.

Laura L. Carstensen is Professor of Psychology and the Fairleigh S. Dickinson Jr. Professor in Public Policy at Stanford University where she serves as founding director of the Stanford Center on Longevity. Dr. Carstensen's research has been supported continuously by the National Institute on Aging for more than 25 years and she is currently supported through a prestigious MERIT Award. In 2011, she authored the book, A Long Bright Future: Happiness, Health, and Financial Security in an Age of Increased Longevity. Dr. Carstensen has served on the National Advisory Council on Aging and the MacArthur Foundation's Research Network on an Aging Society. In 2016, she was inducted into the National Academy of Medicine. She has won numerous awards, including the Kleemeier Award from the Gerontological Society of America, a Guggenheim fellowship, and the Master Mentor Award from the American Psychological Association. She received a B.S.from the University of Rochester and Ph.D. in clinical psychology from West Virginia University.

Martha Deevy joined the Stanford Center on Longevity in January 2009 and serves as Associate Director and Senior Research Scholar. While at the Center, Martha has led the financial security research program which has focused efforts on retirement readiness, working longer and the detection and prevention of fraud. Prior to joining Stanford, Martha had a long career with Silicon Valley firms. She has held positions in business development, strategic planning, finance, product development and IT and held senior executive positions at Apple, Charles Schwab and Intuit. She has served on the boards of directors of a number of publicly traded and non-profit organizations and is currently the vice-chair for the SPOON Foundation, which serves nutritionally underserved children. She received an M.B.A. in Finance and Management Information Systems from University of Minnesota and a B.A. in Economics from University of Illinois.

Theodore M. Homa, MD, CMD, is an internal medicine/gerontology specialist with over 49 years of experience. Between his internship and residency, he served in the US Navy. In addition to his medical practice, Dr. Homa is a guest speaker at conferences. Dr. Homa authored Archimedes' Claw, which is the story of a professor who figures out the key to time travel. From life as a successful doctor to his life-altering experience with congestive heart failure and an eventual heart transplant, Dr Homa brings an unparalleled breadth of knowledge and experience.

Jay Jackson, President & CEO of Abacus Life, is a highly experienced alternative asset manager. Jay joined Abacus Life in 2016 and was named President & CEO in 2018. Jay has diverse high-level financial sector experience, including fund development and directing major portfolios and investor processes. Jay is an acknowledged excellent leader with a focus on maximizing value, service, and awareness, which, taken together, led to Abacus Life's incredible growth.

Matteo Leombroni is a Ph.D. student in Economics at Stanford University. He is interested in macroeconomics and finance. He is currently collaborating with the European Central Bank (ECB) working on asset allocation of pension and insurance funds. Before starting his Ph.D., he worked as an Analyst at Goldman Sachs for the European Economics team in London. He earned a BSc in Economics from LUISS University and a MSc in Finance from Bocconi University.

Derek Prusa is an Investment Adviser representative of Aspire Investment Advisory, LLC, a Michigan Registered Investment Adviser. Prior to starting Aspire Wealth to work with individuals, he was a key employee at one of the fastest growing private companies in America, where he helped manage over $3.8 billion in total assets. In this role, he was exposed to numerous types of investment strategies, resulting in a strong understanding of what actually works in practice (rather than just on paper). Derek has been a

CFP® professional since 2015, a CFA Charterholder since 2016, and a certified investment nerd since he can remember. In 2015, he was honored to be included in a 30 under 30 list for LifeHealthPro, being named a young professional transforming the industry.

Jialu Streeter joined the Stanford Center on Longevity in 2016 as a Research Scientist. Dr. Streeter is a development macroeconomist interested in the effects of public policies on economic growth, wealth distribution, and welfare. Her research has been published on Southern Economic Journal, Energy Policy, the Chinese Economy, Asian Development Review, and so forth. Most of her work is empirical and utilizes a large amount of microeconomic data. She received a B.A. in Economics and a B.S. in Mathematics from Huazhong University of Science and Technology (HUST) in China, and a M.A. and a Ph.D. in Economics from Indiana University, Bloomington. In her spare time, she is an avid piano player.

Benjamin Webster is an Investment Adviser representative of Aspire Investment Advisory, LLC, a Michigan Registered Investment Adviser. Before starting Aspire Wealth, he led a team of financial planners for one of the fastest-growing private companies in America, where he had the opportunity to work with advisors from all across the United States. Benjamin has been a Certified Financial Planner™ since 2018.

Made in the USA
Las Vegas, NV
29 September 2023